The History of the Caribbean

Island Legends

Copyright © 2023 by Nicole Audrey Foster and Einar Felix Hansen.

All rights reserved. No part of this publication may be reproduced, stored in a retrieval system, or transmitted, in any form or by any means, electronic, mechanical, photocopying, recording, or otherwise, without the prior written permission of the copyright holder. This book was created with the help of Artificial Intelligence technology.

The contents of this book are intended for entertainment purposes only. While every effort has been made to ensure the accuracy and reliability of the information presented, the author and publisher make no warranties or representations as to the accuracy, completeness, or suitability of the information contained herein. The information presented in this book is not intended as a substitute for professional advice, and readers should consult with qualified professionals in the relevant fields for specific advice.

The Caribbean: An Introduction to Paradise 7

The Taino Legacy: Indigenous Peoples of the Caribbean 11

Columbus and the Age of Exploration 14

The Spanish Conquest: From Hispaniola to Cuba 17

Buccaneers and Privateers: Tales of the Sea 20

Sugar and Slavery: The Plantation Economy 24

Pirates of the Caribbean: Legends and Realities 27

The African Diaspora: Cultural Heritage and Resistance 30

The French Connection: Martinique and Guadeloupe 34

The British Empire: Jamaica and Barbados 37

Pirates of the Bahamas: Nassau's Infamous Past 40

The Dutch Influence: Curaçao and Aruba 43

Pirates, Privateers, and Port Royal: Jamaica's Infamous Port 46

The Spanish Main: Treasure Hunting in the Caribbean 49

The Maroons: Freedom Fighters of the Caribbean 52

The Haitian Revolution: Birth of a Nation 55

Cuba Libre: From Spanish Rule to Revolution 58

Puerto Rico: A Tale of Colonization and Identity 61

The Lesser Antilles: Gems of the Caribbean 64

Jamaica: Reggae, Rum, and Rastafarianism 67

Trinidad and Tobago: Carnival and Cultural Fusion 70

Barbados: Sun, Sand, and British Heritage 73

The Dominican Republic: Merengue and Dominicanidad 76

The Bahamas: Paradise Islands and Underwater Wonders 80

Grenada: The Spice Isle of the Caribbean 83

Curaçao: A Dutch Caribbean Jewel 86

St. Kitts and Nevis: The First British Colony in the Caribbean 89

St. Lucia: Pitons, Rainforests, and Creole Culture 92

Antigua and Barbuda: Sailing Capital of the Caribbean 95

St. Vincent and the Grenadines: The Land of the Pirates 99

The Cayman Islands: Tax Havens and Marine Life 102

The British Virgin Islands: Sailors' Paradise 106

The U.S. Virgin Islands: American Caribbean Delights 110

Belize: Barrier Reefs and Ancient Maya Ruins 113

Aruba: One Happy Island in the Caribbean 116

The Turks and Caicos Islands: Hidden Gems of the Caribbean 119

Diving into the Depths: Exploring Caribbean Marine Life 122

Wildlife Wonders: Flora and Fauna of the Caribbean 125

Tropical Temptations: Caribbean Cuisine and Drinks 128

Caribbean Music and Dance: Soca, Calypso, and Reggaeton 131

Caribbean Carnival: Festive Celebrations and Masquerades 134

Preserving Paradise: Sustainable Tourism in the Caribbean 137

Conclusion 141

The Caribbean: An Introduction to Paradise

Nestled amidst the sparkling waters of the Caribbean Sea, the region known as the Caribbean is a tapestry of stunning landscapes, vibrant cultures, and rich histories. It encompasses a vast array of islands, islets, and archipelagos, each with its own unique charm and allure. From the moment one sets foot on these shores, a sense of paradise envelops the senses, inviting exploration and igniting a deep connection with nature and history.

Stretching from the southeastern coast of the United States to the northern coast of South America, the Caribbean is blessed with a tropical climate that boasts warm temperatures year-round. This idyllic climate, characterized by gentle trade winds and abundant sunshine, has made the region a perennial favorite among sun-seeking tourists and travelers.

The Caribbean is renowned for its pristine beaches, with soft powdery sands caressed by the azure waters of the sea. From the pink sands of the Bahamas to the white shores of Aruba, and the black volcanic sands of Saint Lucia, the beaches of the Caribbean are a testament to nature's artistry and an invitation to relax and unwind.

Beyond its breathtaking beaches, the Caribbean boasts a diverse and captivating natural landscape. Lush rainforests carpet the interior of many islands, teeming with exotic flora and fauna. From the dense jungles of Dominica, known as the "Nature Island," to the El Yunque National Forest in Puerto Rico, where the sounds of coquis serenade visitors, the Caribbean's natural beauty is a source of wonder and awe.

Underneath the waves, an aquatic wonderland awaits. The Caribbean Sea is home to one of the world's largest barrier reefs, the Mesoamerican Barrier Reef. This vibrant ecosystem supports an array of marine life, including colorful coral formations, tropical fish, sea turtles, and even majestic creatures such as dolphins and whales. Snorkeling and diving enthusiasts flock to the region to explore this underwater paradise, immersing themselves in a world of vibrant colors and mesmerizing marine biodiversity.

The history of the Caribbean is a captivating tapestry woven with the threads of various civilizations and cultures. The indigenous Taino people inhabited the region long before the arrival of European explorers. Their legacy is still visible in the names of places such as Hispaniola (Haiti and the Dominican Republic), Jamaica, and Cuba. The arrival of Christopher Columbus in 1492 marked the beginning of European colonization and the subsequent waves of conquest, trade, and exploitation that would shape the region's history.

The Caribbean became a focal point of European rivalries, with Spain, France, England, and the Netherlands vying for control over its resources and strategic positions. The era of colonialism brought significant changes to the Caribbean, including the introduction of sugar plantations and the transatlantic slave trade. The labor of enslaved Africans, alongside indigenous and European populations, fueled the region's economic prosperity but also sowed the seeds of social and cultural complexities that endure to this day.

Pirates and privateers, such as the infamous Henry Morgan and Blackbeard, roamed the Caribbean's waters, creating legends that still captivate imaginations. These seafaring adventurers exploited the strategic location of the Caribbean, preying upon merchant ships and disrupting colonial trade routes. The notorious Port Royal in Jamaica became a hub for pirate activity, earning the nickname "the Wickedest City on Earth."

In the late 18th century, the Caribbean witnessed transformative events that would shape its destiny. The Haitian Revolution stands as a testament to the strength and resilience of the enslaved population, as they fought for and achieved their independence from France in 1804, becoming the first independent Black republic in the world. The echoes of this revolution reverberated throughout the Caribbean, inspiring other movements for freedom and self-determination.

Throughout the 20th century, the Caribbean saw significant political and cultural shifts. Many islands gained their independence from colonial powers, forging their own paths and identities. The region's cultural tapestry evolved, blending indigenous, African, European, and Asian influences into vibrant expressions of music, dance, art, and cuisine. From the pulsating rhythms of reggae in Jamaica to the lively steel pan music of Trinidad and Tobago, the sounds of the Caribbean resonate far beyond its shores.

Today, tourism plays a vital role in the Caribbean's economy, attracting millions of visitors each year. Travelers flock to the region for its natural beauty, historical sites, and cultural experiences. From luxury resorts and all-inclusive getaways to eco-tourism adventures and immersive cultural exchanges, the Caribbean offers a diverse range of options to suit every traveler's desires.

As we embark on this journey through the history of the Caribbean, we will delve into the ancient and medieval roots of its civilizations, trace the impact of colonization and slavery, explore the struggles for independence and self-determination, and celebrate the vibrant cultures that have blossomed in this tropical paradise. From the shores of Cuba and Puerto Rico to the hidden gems of the Lesser Antilles, the islands of the Caribbean have stories to tell, secrets to unveil, and a timeless allure that continues to captivate the hearts and minds of those who venture into its embrace.

The Taino Legacy: Indigenous Peoples of the Caribbean

Long before the arrival of European explorers, the islands of the Caribbean were inhabited by indigenous peoples who had established vibrant and complex societies. Among these native inhabitants were the Taino people, who left an indelible mark on the history, culture, and heritage of the region. Their legacy serves as a testament to the rich and diverse civilizations that thrived in the Caribbean long before the era of colonization.

The Taino people, also known as the Arawak, were part of a larger indigenous group that inhabited a vast territory spanning from present-day Venezuela and the Guianas to the Greater Antilles and the Bahamas. They were skilled navigators, traversing the waters of the Caribbean in large canoes known as canoas, which allowed them to explore and settle many of the islands in the archipelago.

The Taino society was organized into chiefdoms, with caciques (chiefs) leading their respective communities. These caciques held positions of authority and were responsible for making decisions concerning the welfare of their people. The Taino had a hierarchical social structure, with nobles, commoners, and slaves comprising different strata of society.

Agriculture formed the foundation of the Taino's subsistence. They cultivated staple crops such as maize (corn), yuca (cassava), sweet potatoes, and various fruits, which provided sustenance for their communities. They practiced advanced farming techniques, including the cultivation of raised beds called conucos and the use of a system known as coa, a wooden tool used for digging and planting.

The Taino also had a deep spiritual connection with nature, which influenced every aspect of their lives. They believed in a complex pantheon of deities and spirits, with the supreme god known as Yúcahu, the giver of cassava, being highly revered. Ceremonies and rituals played a significant role in Taino culture, with offerings, songs, dances, and the consumption of a fermented beverage called casabe used to communicate with the spiritual realm.

Artistic expression was another integral part of Taino culture. They crafted intricate pottery, often adorned with intricate geometric designs and representations of animals and mythological figures. Stone carvings known as zemis, which depicted spiritual beings, were also highly valued. These artistic creations showcased the Taino's craftsmanship and reflected their worldview and spiritual beliefs.

The Taino had a keen understanding of their natural surroundings and made use of the abundant resources provided by the Caribbean environment. They were skilled fishermen, using nets, spears, and hooks to catch fish and other marine creatures. The sea not only provided sustenance but also served as a vital transportation network, connecting different islands and facilitating trade among the Taino communities.

European contact with the Taino began with Christopher Columbus's arrival in the Caribbean in 1492. The initial encounters between the Taino and the Europeans were marked by curiosity, exchange, and cultural misunderstandings. However, the subsequent waves of colonization and the harsh realities of the encomienda system, which exploited indigenous labor, led to significant changes in Taino society.

The Taino population suffered greatly from the arrival of European diseases, to which they had little immunity. The introduction of forced labor, along with the disruption of their traditional way of life, resulted in a decline in Taino populations across the Caribbean. Many Taino communities were decimated, and their cultural practices and languages were suppressed or lost over time.

Despite these challenges, the Taino legacy endures in the Caribbean. Efforts to reclaim and revitalize Taino culture have been undertaken by modern-day descendants and indigenous communities, seeking to reconnect with their ancestral roots. Through archaeological excavations, linguistic studies, and the preservation of traditional knowledge, the Taino's contributions to the Caribbean's cultural heritage are being acknowledged and celebrated.

The Taino legacy serves as a reminder of the vibrant indigenous civilizations that once flourished in the Caribbean. Their agricultural practices, spiritual beliefs, artistic expressions, and navigational skills are testament to their ingenuity and adaptability. By acknowledging and honoring the Taino's historical presence, we can gain a deeper understanding of the Caribbean's rich cultural tapestry and recognize the enduring legacies of its indigenous peoples.

Columbus and the Age of Exploration

The Age of Exploration, a pivotal period in world history, saw European sailors embark on daring voyages of discovery, forever changing the course of human civilization. At the forefront of this era was the Italian explorer Christopher Columbus, whose voyages across the Atlantic Ocean opened up new possibilities and ignited a wave of exploration in the late 15th century.

Born in Genoa, Italy, around 1451, Columbus was driven by a fervent desire to find a westward route to Asia, particularly to the lucrative spice trade. With the financial backing of Queen Isabella of Castile and King Ferdinand of Aragon, Columbus set sail on his first voyage on August 3, 1492, aboard the Santa Maria, accompanied by the Pinta and the Niña.

After a long and arduous journey, Columbus and his crew made landfall on an island in the present-day Bahamas, which he named San Salvador. This momentous event marked the "discovery" of the Americas by Europeans, although it is important to note that indigenous peoples had already inhabited these lands for thousands of years.

Columbus's subsequent voyages, spanning from 1493 to 1504, expanded European knowledge of the Caribbean and the Americas. He explored various islands in the Caribbean, including present-day Cuba, Hispaniola (shared by Haiti and the Dominican Republic), Jamaica, and Puerto Rico. These expeditions not only paved the way for further European colonization but also initiated a significant exchange of goods, plants, animals, and diseases between the Old World and the New World.

One of Columbus's notable contributions was the establishment of Spanish colonies in the Caribbean. In 1493, he founded the settlement of La Isabela on the island of Hispaniola, which served as the first European outpost in the Americas. The subsequent colonization efforts led to the introduction of European livestock, crops, and technologies to the Caribbean, while also resulting in the forced labor and mistreatment of indigenous populations.

The encounters between Columbus and the indigenous peoples of the Caribbean were complex and varied. While some indigenous groups initially welcomed the arrival of the Europeans, hoping to establish trade and diplomatic relations, the subsequent actions of the Europeans, including forced labor and the spread of diseases, led to significant conflicts and resistance from the native populations.

It is important to note that Columbus's arrival in the Caribbean had far-reaching consequences for the indigenous peoples. European diseases, such as smallpox and measles, to which the indigenous populations had no immunity, caused devastating epidemics, resulting in a significant decline in their numbers. The Europeans also exploited the labor of the indigenous peoples, subjecting them to harsh conditions and enslavement.

The voyages of Columbus and the subsequent European exploration of the Americas were driven by a complex mix of motivations, including economic gain, political rivalries, and a thirst for knowledge and adventure. The voyages opened up new trade routes, expanded European empires, and sparked a profound transformation in global commerce, culture, and the exchange of ideas.

Columbus's voyages were just the beginning of a broader European colonization of the Americas, with other explorers, such as John Cabot, Amerigo Vespucci, and Ferdinand Magellan, following in his footsteps. The Age of Exploration ushered in an era of unprecedented global interconnectedness, but it also brought immense human suffering and disrupted the existing social and cultural fabric of the indigenous populations.

While Columbus's role in history remains controversial, his voyages undeniably had a profound and lasting impact on the world. The exploration and colonization of the Americas laid the foundation for the rise of European empires, the transatlantic slave trade, and the forging of new identities in the Americas. It is a complex and multifaceted chapter in human history, one that continues to be examined and debated as we seek to understand the legacies of this era of exploration and its ongoing repercussions.

The Spanish Conquest: From Hispaniola to Cuba

The Spanish conquest of the Caribbean islands was a pivotal chapter in the history of the region. Following Christopher Columbus's initial arrival in the late 15th century, Spanish explorers and conquistadors set their sights on further exploration, conquest, and colonization. Led by figures such as Diego Velázquez and Hernán Cortés, the Spanish rapidly expanded their presence, leaving an indelible mark on the islands of Hispaniola and Cuba.

After Columbus's first voyage in 1492, the Spanish crown sought to solidify its control over the newly discovered territories. In 1496, Bartholomew Columbus, Christopher's brother, established the first Spanish colony on Hispaniola, naming it La Isabela. However, due to a combination of factors, including disease, harsh conditions, and conflicts with indigenous populations, the colony struggled and was eventually abandoned.

In 1499, Diego Velázquez, a Spanish conquistador, arrived in Hispaniola and was appointed governor by the Spanish crown. Velázquez established a new settlement on the southern coast of the island, which he named Santo Domingo. Under Velázquez's leadership, Santo Domingo thrived, becoming the first permanent European settlement in the Americas.

From Hispaniola, the Spanish began their expansion to neighboring islands, most notably Cuba. In 1509, Velázquez led an expedition to Cuba and established the settlement of Baracoa, the island's first Spanish settlement. Over time, more Spanish settlements were founded, including Santiago de Cuba and Havana, as the Spanish sought to exploit Cuba's abundant natural resources, such as gold, tobacco, and sugar.

The Spanish conquest of these islands was marked by a combination of military force, alliances with indigenous groups, and the introduction of European diseases, which had a devastating impact on the native populations. The indigenous Taíno peoples of Hispaniola and Cuba, already weakened by earlier encounters with European diseases, faced further challenges as the Spanish sought to extract resources and establish control over the land.

Spanish colonization brought significant changes to the islands' social, economic, and cultural landscapes. The Spanish introduced the encomienda system, which granted Spanish settlers control over indigenous labor and tribute, leading to the exploitation and mistreatment of the indigenous populations. The colonizers also introduced European crops, such as sugarcane, and livestock, transforming the islands' agricultural practices and initiating the development of large-scale plantations.

The Spanish presence in Hispaniola and Cuba sparked resistance from indigenous populations. In Hispaniola, the Taíno people, led by Chief Enriquillo, engaged in a protracted conflict against the Spanish in the early 16th century. In Cuba, the resistance was led by Chief Hatuey, who organized indigenous groups to resist Spanish domination. While these resistance movements ultimately failed to halt Spanish control, they represent the resilience and determination of the indigenous populations in the face of colonization.

The conquest of Hispaniola and Cuba also served as a launching point for further Spanish expeditions and conquests in the Americas. Hernán Cortés, who initially served under Velázquez in Cuba, set out from the island to conquer the Aztec Empire in Mexico. This conquest brought immense wealth to the Spanish crown and further solidified Spanish dominance in the region.

The Spanish conquest of Hispaniola and Cuba shaped the trajectory of the Caribbean and the Americas as a whole. It established the foundation for Spanish colonial rule, ushering in a period of extensive exploitation, colonization, and cultural transformation. The legacy of Spanish colonization, both positive and negative, can still be seen in the languages, traditions, and social structures of the Caribbean islands today.

Buccaneers and Privateers: Tales of the Sea

The era of buccaneers and privateers in the Caribbean is a captivating chapter in maritime history. These seafaring adventurers, often depicted as romanticized figures or feared pirates, played a significant role in the geopolitical struggles and economic interests of the 17th and 18th centuries. This chapter explores the tales of the buccaneers and privateers who roamed the Caribbean Sea, leaving a lasting legacy on the region's history.

Buccaneers were a distinct group of hunters and adventurers who operated in the Caribbean during the 17th century. Originating from the French word "boucan," meaning a wooden frame used for smoking meat, the buccaneers were primarily hunters who smoked meat, known as "boucan," for provisions. Their skills in hunting wild cattle and pigs provided them with sustenance and an economic opportunity.

The buccaneers' activities, however, extended beyond hunting. They possessed intimate knowledge of the Caribbean's intricate waterways, making them adept sailors and navigators. Taking advantage of their seafaring abilities, the buccaneers turned to piracy, attacking Spanish ships and coastal settlements to acquire wealth and goods. Their raids often targeted Spanish colonies, as Spain held a dominant position in the region and possessed vast wealth from its New World colonies.

The buccaneers established bases on islands such as Tortuga (off the coast of present-day Haiti) and Port

Royal (in present-day Jamaica). From these bases, they launched daring attacks on Spanish galleons, disrupting the Spanish Empire's lucrative trade routes and weakening its hold on the Caribbean.

The buccaneers were known for their distinctive methods and tactics. They employed swift and maneuverable vessels, known as "fast ships," that allowed them to outrun larger Spanish ships. These ships were often heavily armed with cannons and equipped with smaller, more agile boats known as "barcolettes" or "longboats" for boarding enemy vessels.

Some notable buccaneer leaders gained legendary status for their exploits. François l'Olonnais, a French buccaneer, was infamous for his brutality and audacity. He is said to have captured the Spanish city of Maracaibo in present-day Venezuela, amassing great wealth. Another renowned figure was Henry Morgan, a Welsh privateer who became the governor of Jamaica. Morgan successfully plundered several Spanish settlements, including the sack of Panama City in 1671.

The distinction between buccaneers and privateers is worth noting. While buccaneers were essentially pirates, privateers were authorized by their respective governments to carry out acts of piracy against enemy nations during times of war. These privateers, holding official letters of marque or commissions, essentially operated as legalized pirates, sanctioned by their governments to disrupt enemy commerce and weaken their adversaries.

The European powers, including England, France, and the Netherlands, often issued these letters of marque to privateers, granting them the right to attack and seize enemy ships and goods. Privateering became a lucrative enterprise, attracting sailors, merchants, and investors who sought to profit from the spoils of war.

The privateers played a significant role in the geopolitical struggles among European powers in the Caribbean. They targeted not only Spanish vessels but also those of rival European nations. These acts of piracy and privateering intensified during times of conflict, such as the Anglo-Spanish War, the War of the Spanish Succession, and the various conflicts between European powers vying for supremacy in the region.

The privateers' activities had far-reaching consequences. They disrupted trade and weakened the economic power of their enemies. However, their actions also contributed to the destabilization of the Caribbean region, leading to conflicts and tensions between European powers and impacting the local populations caught in the crossfire.

As the European powers solidified their control over the Caribbean, the buccaneering and privateering activities gradually declined. The emergence of stronger naval forces and the shifting political dynamics in Europe brought an end to the golden age of piracy and privateering in the Caribbean.

The tales of the buccaneers and privateers continue to capture the imagination, serving as the inspiration for countless books, movies, and legends. They embody the spirit of adventure, rebellion, and the relentless pursuit of wealth and freedom on the high seas. While their activities were often driven by personal gain, their exploits and the challenges they faced reveal the complex interplay of power, politics, and maritime warfare in the Caribbean during this tumultuous period.

The era of buccaneers and privateers in the Caribbean serves as a reminder of the region's strategic significance, its rich maritime history, and the enduring fascination with these seafaring legends. The stories of their adventures continue to intrigue and captivate, reminding us of the complexities and allure of life on the open seas during a time when the Caribbean was a playground for those seeking both riches and infamy.

Sugar and Slavery: The Plantation Economy

The establishment of the plantation economy, driven by the production of sugar, played a significant role in shaping the history of the Caribbean. This chapter delves into the complex and intertwined relationship between sugar production and the institution of slavery, exploring the economic, social, and cultural impact of this pivotal era.

Sugar, originally introduced to the Caribbean by Christopher Columbus on his second voyage, rapidly became the region's most profitable and sought-after commodity. The Caribbean's tropical climate and fertile soil were ideal for cultivating sugarcane, a labor-intensive crop that required large plantations, abundant labor, and a complex system of production.

The plantation system revolved around the cultivation, processing, and exportation of sugarcane. Vast tracts of land were cleared and transformed into plantations, with fields of sugarcane stretching as far as the eye could see. The plantation owners, often of European descent, established a hierarchical social structure, where wealth and power were concentrated in the hands of a privileged few.

The cultivation of sugarcane was an arduous and labor-intensive process. Enslaved Africans were forcibly brought to the Caribbean to provide the labor required for sugarcane cultivation and processing. These enslaved individuals endured immense suffering, as they were subjected to grueling work conditions, harsh punishments, and the dehumanizing realities of slavery.

The production process involved several stages. The land was cleared and prepared for planting, and young sugarcane shoots were planted in carefully spaced rows. As the sugarcane matured, it was harvested and transported to the sugar mills, where it was crushed to extract the juice. The juice was then boiled in large cauldrons to remove impurities and reduce it to a thick syrup. Finally, the syrup was dried and granulated to produce raw sugar, which was then refined into various grades of white sugar.

The plantation owners amassed great wealth from the production and exportation of sugar. The Caribbean became a global hub of sugar production, supplying Europe, the Americas, and other parts of the world with this highly valued commodity. The profitability of sugar cultivation led to the expansion of plantations and the acquisition of more enslaved labor, perpetuating a system of exploitation and cruelty.

The plantation economy had profound social and cultural ramifications in the Caribbean. The plantations created a racially stratified society, with people of African descent comprising the majority of the enslaved population, while the European plantation owners held the power and wealth. This racial division and hierarchy would leave a lasting impact on the region's social structures and continue to shape identities and inequalities to this day.

The impact of the plantation economy extended beyond the confines of the Caribbean. It influenced global trade patterns, as the demand for sugar led to the development of complex networks of commerce and exchange. The profits generated from sugar production contributed to the economic growth and industrial development of Europe, helping to fuel the expansion of capitalist systems and the rise of modern capitalism.

The legacy of the plantation economy and the institution of slavery is a painful and complex one. Slavery was a brutal system that stripped enslaved Africans of their dignity, rights, and freedom. It caused immense suffering and trauma, leaving a deep and lasting scar on the Caribbean and the descendants of those who endured its horrors.

While the plantation economy was eventually challenged and dismantled through various movements, including abolitionism and the fight for emancipation, its impact on the Caribbean's social, economic, and cultural fabric cannot be understated. The struggles and resistance of enslaved individuals, alongside the efforts of abolitionists and freedom fighters, were instrumental in bringing an end to the system of slavery and laying the foundation for the ongoing fight for equality and justice.

The history of the sugar and slavery in the Caribbean is a complex and multi-layered narrative. It is a reminder of the interconnectedness of global trade, the enduring consequences of exploitation, and the resilience of those who fought against oppression. Understanding this history is crucial in acknowledging the painful past, addressing the present-day legacies of inequality, and working towards a more just and inclusive future.

Pirates of the Caribbean: Legends and Realities

The tales of pirates in the Caribbean have captured the imaginations of people for centuries. From swashbuckling adventures to buried treasure, these legends have become intertwined with the region's rich maritime history. This chapter delves into the realities and myths surrounding the pirates of the Caribbean, exploring their motivations, activities, and the lasting impact of their presence.

Piracy in the Caribbean reached its peak during the 17th and 18th centuries. The region's strategic location, with its numerous islands, hidden coves, and bustling trade routes, made it an ideal haven for pirates seeking wealth and adventure. However, it is important to note that piracy was not exclusive to the Caribbean and was prevalent in other parts of the world as well.

The term "pirate" often conjures up images of individuals who sailed the seas, flying the Jolly Roger and attacking unsuspecting vessels. However, it is crucial to differentiate between pirates and privateers. Pirates were outlaws who engaged in acts of robbery and violence without legal authorization, while privateers were individuals who held letters of marque or commissions from their respective governments, authorizing them to attack and seize enemy ships during times of war. The life of a pirate was a dangerous and uncertain one. Pirates hailed from various backgrounds, including former sailors, escaped slaves, and disenfranchised individuals seeking a life outside the constraints of society. They formed loose associations or bands known as pirate crews, which operated under their own rules and elected their captains through democratic processes.

Pirates targeted a wide range of vessels, including merchant ships, naval vessels, and even coastal towns. They utilized a variety of tactics to overpower their victims, including surprise attacks, intimidation, and the use of superior firepower. Their ships, such as the famous pirate sloops and brigantines, were often fast and maneuverable, allowing them to outmaneuver larger and slower vessels.

The Caribbean pirates had various base locations where they could rest, refit their ships, and divide their spoils. These bases, often located on remote islands or in hidden coves, served as safe havens. Among the notorious pirate havens were Port Royal in Jamaica, Nassau in the Bahamas, and Tortuga off the coast of present-day Haiti. These bases provided pirates with the opportunity to socialize, trade goods, and recruit new crew members.

Contrary to popular belief, not all pirates buried their treasure. While there have been instances of pirates stashing away their plunder in hidden locations, such as on secluded islands or in remote caves, burying treasure was not a widespread practice. Pirates were more likely to squander their loot through extravagant spending, gambling, or investing in legitimate businesses, as they sought to enjoy the fruits of their illicit activities.

The Caribbean pirates were not all cut from the same cloth. Some gained notoriety for their ruthlessness and brutality, while others developed a reputation for showing leniency and even adhering to their own codes of conduct. Notable pirates in the Caribbean included Blackbeard (Edward Teach), Calico Jack Rackham, Anne Bonny, and Mary

Read. These individuals, along with many others, have become the stuff of legends, their stories passed down through generations.

Naval authorities and European powers regarded piracy as a menace and sought to suppress it. Various naval campaigns, such as the Spanish treasure fleets and the British Royal Navy's efforts, were launched to combat piracy in the Caribbean. These campaigns aimed to protect trade routes, capture or eliminate pirates, and restore order in the region.

The decline of piracy in the Caribbean can be attributed to several factors. Increased naval presence, the enforcement of anti-piracy laws, and changing geopolitical dynamics played significant roles. The end of the Golden Age of Piracy in the early 18th century saw the decline of organized pirate activity, although sporadic incidents continued well into the 19th century.

The legends and myths surrounding the pirates of the Caribbean have endured through literature, movies, and popular culture. They have become symbols of adventure, freedom, and rebellion. While piracy was undoubtedly a criminal and violent enterprise, it is important to recognize that the reality was often more complex, with pirates reflecting the social, political, and economic circumstances of their time.

The stories of the pirates of the Caribbean provide a fascinating glimpse into the region's history and its connections to the broader world of maritime exploration and trade. They serve as a reminder of the complexities of human nature, the allure of the unknown, and the enduring fascination with tales of daring and adventure on the high seas.

The African Diaspora: Cultural Heritage and Resistance

The African Diaspora, resulting from the transatlantic slave trade, represents a profound and enduring chapter in the history of the Caribbean. This chapter explores the cultural heritage and resistance of the African Diaspora, highlighting the resilience, creativity, and contributions of the enslaved Africans and their descendants in shaping the region's rich cultural tapestry.

The transatlantic slave trade forcibly transported millions of Africans from diverse ethnic, linguistic, and cultural backgrounds to the Caribbean. These individuals brought with them a wealth of cultural traditions, knowledge, and skills that would play a significant role in the development of Caribbean societies.

Enslaved Africans faced unimaginable hardships, enduring the brutalities of slavery, separation from their families and homelands, and the denial of their basic human rights. However, even in the face of such adversity, they found ways to maintain and preserve elements of their cultural heritage.

Language was one powerful means through which African cultural heritage persisted. Despite the efforts of slave owners to suppress African languages, enslaved individuals developed unique Creole languages, such as Jamaican Patois and Haitian Creole, blending elements of their native languages with European languages. These Creole languages continue to be spoken in the Caribbean, serving as a testament to the resilience and creativity of the African Diaspora.

Music and dance were also integral to the preservation of African cultural heritage. Enslaved Africans used their musical traditions, rhythms, and instruments to express their emotions, communicate, and maintain a sense of identity. From the vibrant sounds of reggae in Jamaica to the rhythmic beats of Afro-Cuban music and the lively dances of the Dominican Republic's merengue, African influences are deeply embedded in the Caribbean's musical and dance traditions.

Religion played a crucial role in the cultural resilience of the African Diaspora. Enslaved Africans brought their diverse religious beliefs and practices, which often blended with Christianity or other colonial religions. In the Caribbean, syncretic religions emerged, such as Vodou in Haiti, Santería in Cuba, and Obeah in Jamaica, which combine African spiritual beliefs with elements of Catholicism and indigenous traditions. These syncretic religions became vital channels for maintaining cultural identity, spirituality, and resistance against oppressive systems.

The visual arts and crafts of the African Diaspora also thrived despite the limitations imposed by slavery. African artistic traditions found expression in pottery, basket weaving, woodcarving, and other crafts. These artistic creations often incorporated symbolic motifs, patterns, and designs inspired by African heritage, enriching the visual aesthetics of the Caribbean and serving as a powerful form of cultural expression.

Resistance was a central aspect of the African Diaspora's history. Enslaved Africans and their descendants employed various forms of resistance, ranging from acts of open rebellion to subtle acts of everyday defiance. Slave revolts, such as the Haitian Revolution, led by Toussaint Louverture, and the Morant Bay Rebellion in Jamaica, challenged the institution of slavery and shook the foundations of colonial power.

Maroons, communities of escaped slaves who established autonomous settlements in remote and rugged areas, represented another form of resistance. These resilient communities, such as the Jamaican Maroons and the Windward Maroons of Dominica, maintained their cultural traditions, built independent societies, and mounted guerilla warfare against colonial forces.

The African Diaspora's resistance extended beyond armed uprisings and maroon communities. Everyday acts of resistance, such as cultural preservation, the practice of African traditions in secret, and the maintenance of kinship networks, were forms of defiance against the dehumanizing effects of slavery. These acts played a significant role in preserving African cultural heritage and laying the foundation for future generations to reclaim their identity.

The legacy of the African Diaspora is evident in the Caribbean's cultural landscape today. African influences permeate the music, dance, language, religion, and artistic expressions of the region. From the vibrant celebrations of Carnival to the powerful rhythms of drumming and the symbolism in traditional ceremonies, the African heritage of the Caribbean is celebrated and embraced.

The cultural heritage and resistance of the African Diaspora continue to shape the identities of Caribbean nations and their diasporic communities around the world. They serve as a testament to the strength, resilience, and indomitable spirit of the African ancestors and their descendants. Recognizing and honoring this heritage is crucial for understanding the complexities of Caribbean history and appreciating the diverse cultures that have emerged from the African Diaspora.

The French Connection: Martinique and Guadeloupe

The islands of Martinique and Guadeloupe, known as the French West Indies, have a rich and complex history that intertwines French colonial influence with the vibrant cultures of the Caribbean. This chapter explores the French connection to Martinique and Guadeloupe, examining the historical, social, and cultural aspects that have shaped these islands.

The French first arrived in the Caribbean in the early 17th century, establishing colonies on various islands, including Martinique and Guadeloupe. These islands, located in the Lesser Antilles, provided favorable conditions for the cultivation of cash crops such as sugarcane and coffee. The French recognized the economic potential of these islands and sought to exploit their resources.

The plantation economy thrived in Martinique and Guadeloupe, with sugarcane being the primary crop. Large plantations, known as estates, covered the landscapes, worked by enslaved Africans and later by indentured laborers from other parts of the world. The French introduced a strict social hierarchy, with plantation owners at the top and enslaved laborers at the bottom.

The French colonial administration played a significant role in governing the islands. Martinique and Guadeloupe were considered overseas departments of France, granting them the same status as any other department within the

French Republic. This meant that the islands were integrated into the French legal, political, and economic systems. The French language, legal framework, and administrative structures became deeply ingrained in the islands' societies.

The influence of France is evident in the architecture, cuisine, and cultural traditions of Martinique and Guadeloupe. The cities and towns feature colonial-era buildings with French architectural styles, such as ornate balconies and shuttered windows. French culinary traditions, including the use of French ingredients and cooking techniques, blend with local flavors and ingredients to create a unique Caribbean-French fusion cuisine. This fusion is exemplified by dishes like accras (salt cod fritters) and colombo (a spicy curry dish).

French culture and language are an integral part of the islands' identity. French is the official language, and education is conducted in French. However, Creole languages, influenced by African and other languages, are widely spoken as a reflection of the islands' diverse heritage. These Creole languages serve as vehicles of cultural expression, reinforcing a distinct cultural identity that is both rooted in the French tradition and shaped by the local Caribbean context.

The islands of Martinique and Guadeloupe have also produced notable literary and artistic figures who have contributed to French and Caribbean cultural landscapes. Writers and poets such as Aimé Césaire, Édouard Glissant, and Maryse Condé have emerged from these islands, exploring themes of identity, colonialism, and the complexities of Caribbean life. Their works have gained international recognition and have shed light on the unique experiences of being both French and Caribbean.

The history of Martinique and Guadeloupe has not been without challenges and tensions. The legacy of slavery, colonialism, and social inequalities has influenced the islands' social and political dynamics. Movements for independence, cultural autonomy, and social justice have emerged, seeking to address the legacies of the past and advocate for a more equitable future.

Martinique and Guadeloupe continue to maintain strong ties with France, benefiting from economic support, educational opportunities, and cultural exchanges. The islands enjoy representation in the French Parliament, and their residents are French citizens. This connection provides the islands with access to the resources and advantages of being part of the European Union.

The French connection to Martinique and Guadeloupe is multifaceted, embodying both the complexities of colonial history and the enduring cultural ties between the islands and France. The islands' French heritage, blended with their vibrant Caribbean traditions, has created a unique cultural milieu that celebrates diversity and fosters a sense of belonging.

The British Empire: Jamaica and Barbados

Jamaica and Barbados, two prominent islands in the Caribbean, bear the imprint of the British Empire, which shaped their histories, societies, and cultures. This chapter delves into the British connection to Jamaica and Barbados, exploring their colonial past, the impact of British rule, and the legacies that persist to this day.

British involvement in Jamaica and Barbados began in the 17th century when both islands were settled by the English. Barbados was the first to be colonized, with English settlers arriving in 1627. It quickly became a hub of sugar production, driven by the labor of enslaved Africans. Jamaica, on the other hand, was initially occupied by the Spanish but came under British control in 1655.

The plantation system, with its reliance on enslaved labor, thrived in both Jamaica and Barbados under British rule. Sugar cane became the primary crop, and vast plantations dominated the landscapes, worked by thousands of enslaved Africans who endured unimaginable suffering and exploitation. The labor-intensive nature of sugar production led to the importation of enslaved Africans on a large scale, significantly shaping the demographic composition of both islands. British colonial administration established control over Jamaica and Barbados, introducing legal, political, and economic systems that reflected British institutions. These islands became part of the British Empire, with governance carried out through appointed governors and legislative bodies. The English language, British customs, and legal frameworks became deeply ingrained in the islands' societies.

The British influence is evident in the architectural styles and infrastructure of Jamaica and Barbados. Plantation great houses, often with Georgian or Victorian architectural designs, dot the landscapes, serving as reminders of the colonial past. Historic sites such as Port Royal in Jamaica, known as the "wickedest city on earth" during its heyday, and Bridgetown in Barbados, a UNESCO World Heritage Site, bear witness to the islands' historical significance.

British cultural traditions also left an indelible mark on Jamaica and Barbados. The English language became the dominant means of communication, and British customs, such as cricket and tea-drinking, became part of the islands' social fabric. Education, modeled after the British system, played a crucial role in shaping the islands' intellectual development.

Resistance and rebellion were integral to the islands' history under British rule. Enslaved Africans and their descendants fought against the oppressive system of slavery through acts of resistance, including slave revolts and acts of sabotage. Notable rebellions, such as the Tacky's Revolt in Jamaica in 1760 and the Bussa Rebellion in Barbados in 1816, demonstrated the determination of the enslaved population to secure their freedom.

In the early 19th century, the British Empire abolished the transatlantic slave trade and eventually emancipated enslaved individuals throughout its colonies. The process of emancipation varied between Jamaica and Barbados. Jamaica witnessed a long and complex journey toward full emancipation, which was achieved in 1838, while Barbados embraced a system of apprenticeship before full emancipation in 1834.

The legacies of British colonialism in Jamaica and Barbados continue to shape these islands' socio-economic and political landscapes. The plantation economy, with its deep-rooted social and economic inequalities, has left a lasting impact. The islands grappled with the challenges of transitioning from a slave-based economy to one driven by other sectors, such as agriculture, tourism, and services.

Jamaica and Barbados, as former British colonies, maintain ties with the United Kingdom through their status as members of the Commonwealth. They enjoy political and economic cooperation, educational exchanges, and cultural connections. These connections provide opportunities for trade, investment, and the sharing of resources and expertise. The British Empire's influence on Jamaica and Barbados is a complex and multifaceted aspect of their histories. It is characterized by both the exploitation and suffering endured under the plantation system and the resilience, creativity, and cultural fusion that emerged from the encounter between British and Caribbean traditions.

Recognizing the impact of the British Empire is crucial for understanding the complexities of Jamaica and Barbados' past and present. It allows us to appreciate the cultural diversity, resilience, and contributions of the islands' inhabitants, and fosters a deeper understanding of the legacies of colonization in the Caribbean.

Pirates of the Bahamas: Nassau's Infamous Past

Nassau, the capital of the Bahamas, holds a fascinating place in the history of piracy. This chapter delves into the notorious past of Nassau as a haven for pirates, exploring the factors that contributed to its reputation, the activities of pirates in the region, and the legacy that remains ingrained in the city's identity.

During the "Golden Age of Piracy" in the 17th and 18th centuries, Nassau served as a sanctuary for pirates operating in the Caribbean. The strategic location of the Bahamas, with its numerous islands, hidden coves, and intricate waterways, made it an ideal base for pirates to carry out their activities.

The island of New Providence, where Nassau is situated, became a notorious hub of pirate activity. The lack of a strong British presence and the abundance of natural harbors and secluded bays made it an attractive location for pirates to anchor their ships, restock supplies, and divide their spoils. The absence of a well-established legal system and the corruption of local officials also contributed to the appeal of Nassau for pirates.

Nassau's reputation as a pirate haven was solidified when the island fell into disarray and was essentially abandoned by British authorities. The city became a lawless enclave where pirates and other outlaws could operate with relative impunity. Pirates, such as Benjamin Hornigold, Edward Teach (Blackbeard), and Charles Vane, were among those who frequented Nassau during this time. Pirates in Nassau engaged in a wide range of activities, including attacking and plundering merchant vessels, smuggling goods, and participating in illicit trades. They used the island as a base to plan their raids and divide their spoils. The pirate crews would often gather in Nassau's taverns, such as the infamous Pirate's Republic, to socialize, make alliances, and discuss their next ventures.

The pirates of Nassau operated under their own codes of conduct, known as pirate articles or the "Pirate Code." These codes outlined rules and regulations governing the behavior of pirates, including the distribution of wealth, the treatment of prisoners, and the division of authority among the crew. While adherence to these codes varied, they provided a semblance of order and governance among the pirate crews. The influence of piracy on Nassau's economy cannot be overlooked. The influx of wealth from pirate raids brought economic activity to the city. Pirates spent their loot in local markets, taverns, and brothels, stimulating trade and providing employment opportunities for the local population. Nassau experienced a transient and diverse population, with pirates, merchants, prostitutes, and other individuals seeking opportunities amidst the lawlessness.

The reputation of Nassau as a pirate haven began to decline in the early 18th century. The British government decided to crack down on piracy in the region, launching naval campaigns and granting pardons to pirates who chose to abandon their criminal activities. The appointment of Woodes Rogers as the first Royal Governor of the Bahamas in 1718 marked a turning point in Nassau's history. Rogers, with the support of the

British navy, successfully brought order to the island and suppressed piracy.

Despite the end of Nassau's era as a pirate stronghold, the legacy of piracy remains deeply embedded in the city's identity. The stories, legends, and myths of the pirates who once roamed its shores continue to captivate the imaginations of locals and visitors alike. The city embraces its pirate heritage and recognizes its historical significance as an essential part of its cultural tourism.

Today, Nassau boasts numerous attractions and landmarks associated with its pirate past. The Pirates of Nassau Museum provides visitors with an immersive experience, delving into the world of piracy through interactive exhibits and displays. Forts such as Fort Charlotte and Fort Montagu, built to protect the island from pirate attacks, stand as reminders of Nassau's tumultuous history.

The legacy of piracy in Nassau serves as a reminder of the complexities of the city's history. It encapsulates a period of lawlessness, adventure, and rebellion against the established order. While piracy was undoubtedly a criminal activity, it also represented a challenge to the oppressive systems of colonialism and economic exploitation prevalent during that time.

Nassau's pirate-infused past contributes to its vibrant cultural tapestry, allowing visitors to explore the city's history and engage with the myths and legends that continue to fascinate. It is a testament to the resilience and enduring allure of the pirates of Nassau and their impact on the Bahamas' historical narrative.

The Dutch Influence: Curaçao and Aruba

Curaçao and Aruba, two islands in the Caribbean, bear a distinct Dutch influence that has left an indelible mark on their histories, cultures, and societies. This chapter explores the Dutch connection to Curaçao and Aruba, delving into their colonial past, the impact of Dutch rule, and the enduring legacies that can still be witnessed today.

The Dutch involvement in Curaçao and Aruba began in the early 17th century, when the Dutch West India Company established a presence in the region. These islands, strategically located in the southern Caribbean, became important outposts for the Dutch Empire's ambitions in trade, commerce, and colonial expansion.

Curaçao, in particular, emerged as a significant center of Dutch influence in the Caribbean. The island's natural harbor, Schottegat, provided a safe haven for Dutch ships and facilitated trade with Europe, the Americas, and other parts of the Caribbean. Curaçao became a hub for the Dutch West India Company's operations, serving as a base for commerce, military activities, and slave trading.

Dutch rule in Curaçao and Aruba was characterized by the establishment of plantations, which focused primarily on the cultivation of cash crops such as aloe, cotton, and indigo. The Dutch settlers relied on enslaved Africans as a labor force to work on these plantations, resulting in the development of a highly stratified society.

The Dutch influence on the islands is evident in their architecture, with colorful colonial-style buildings adorning the streets of Willemstad in Curaçao and Oranjestad in Aruba. These buildings showcase Dutch architectural styles, including characteristic gabled roofs, ornate facades, and colorful facades that contribute to the islands' unique visual aesthetics.

Language also reflects the Dutch influence in Curaçao and Aruba. While Papiamento, a Creole language derived from Portuguese, Spanish, Dutch, and African languages, is widely spoken, Dutch is the official language. Dutch education, legal systems, and administrative structures have shaped the islands' governance and institutions.

The Dutch influence extends to cultural traditions and celebrations. Holidays such as King's Day (Koningsdag) and Sinterklaas, a Dutch tradition celebrating Saint Nicholas, are observed and embraced in Curaçao and Aruba. These cultural practices serve as a testament to the enduring ties between the islands and the Netherlands.

Economic development and infrastructure in Curaçao and Aruba have also been influenced by the Dutch presence. The Dutch invested in the development of port facilities, refineries, and tourism infrastructure, contributing to the islands' economic growth and diversification. Both Curaçao and Aruba have developed as tourist destinations, attracting visitors from around the world to experience their natural beauty, vibrant cultures, and Dutch-influenced hospitality.

Political relationships between the Netherlands and Curaçao and Aruba have evolved over time. Today, both islands enjoy a status of autonomy within the Kingdom of the Netherlands. They have their own governments, hold representation in the Dutch Parliament, and have a degree of self-governance in various areas, including tourism, education, and cultural affairs.

The Dutch influence on Curaçao and Aruba is a significant aspect of their identities. It represents a historical connection that has shaped their societies, economies, and cultural landscapes. The islands have embraced their Dutch heritage while also maintaining their unique Caribbean characteristics, resulting in a vibrant fusion of cultures and a sense of diversity that defines their essence.

The Dutch legacy in Curaçao and Aruba is multifaceted, encompassing both positive and challenging aspects. It is important to recognize and understand the complexities of this influence, appreciating the contributions made while also critically examining the impacts of colonialism and the historical legacies that persist.

Curaçao and Aruba stand as reminders of the global interconnectedness of the Dutch Empire and the enduring cultural ties that transcend borders. They embody a fusion of Dutch, Caribbean, and other cultural influences, enriching the region and offering a unique perspective on the tapestry of the Caribbean's history.

Pirates, Privateers, and Port Royal: Jamaica's Infamous Port

Port Royal, a once-infamous port city on the island of Jamaica, holds a captivating place in the history of piracy and privateering. This chapter delves into the maritime exploits that unfolded in Port Royal, exploring the rise of piracy, the activities of privateers, and the allure that made the city notorious throughout the Caribbean.

In the late 17th and early 18th centuries, Port Royal thrived as a bustling hub of trade, commerce, and maritime activities. Its strategic location at the mouth of Kingston Harbor made it an ideal port for ships to resupply, refit, and trade goods. The city's proximity to trade routes and its natural harbor attracted a diverse array of vessels, including merchant ships, naval vessels, and, eventually, pirate and privateer ships.

Piracy flourished in Port Royal during what is known as the "Golden Age of Piracy." The allure of easy wealth and the promise of adventure attracted pirates from all corners of the Caribbean and beyond. Notable pirates, such as Henry Morgan, Calico Jack Rackham, and Anne Bonny, found their way to Port Royal and made it their base of operations.

Pirates in Port Royal engaged in acts of robbery, looting, and violence against ships and coastal towns. They targeted merchant vessels, seizing valuable cargoes and plundering towns along the coast. Port Royal became a hotbed of piracy, with pirates taking advantage of the city's lax security, corrupt officials, and a population willing to trade and profit from their illicit activities.

Privateering also played a significant role in Port Royal's history. Privateers were essentially legalized pirates, operating with the authorization of governments during times of war. These individuals held commissions, known as letters of marque, granting them the right to attack and capture enemy vessels. Port Royal served as a base for privateering activities, with privateers launching attacks against rival European powers and disrupting enemy trade routes.

The activities of pirates and privateers in Port Royal had a significant impact on the city's social and economic dynamics. The influx of wealth from piracy and privateering stimulated trade, led to the growth of businesses, and attracted a diverse population seeking opportunities amidst the lawlessness. The city became a melting pot of cultures, with sailors, merchants, craftsmen, and sex workers establishing a vibrant and cosmopolitan community.

Port Royal's reputation as a den of vice and debauchery also grew. The city was notorious for its raucous taverns, gambling dens, and brothels. It gained a reputation as the "Sodom of the New World," known for its excessive drinking, promiscuity, and lawlessness. The presence of pirates and privateers, with their tales of adventure and wealth, further added to the city's allure and infamy.

However, Port Royal's notoriety was short-lived. In 1692, a devastating earthquake struck the city, causing much of it to sink into the sea. The earthquake, along with subsequent fires and hurricanes, decimated Port Royal, resulting in the loss of countless lives and significant destruction. The disaster marked the end of Port Royal's reign as a hub of piracy and privateering.

Today, Port Royal stands as a small fishing village, its glory days long past. However, the remnants of its intriguing history can still be found. Archaeological excavations have unearthed artifacts and structures that offer glimpses into the city's vibrant past. The Port Royal Archaeological Site serves as a window into the world of pirates, privateers, and the bustling maritime trade that once defined the city.

The legacy of piracy and privateering in Port Royal is a reminder of the complex interplay between law and lawlessness, the pursuit of wealth, and the allure of adventure. It serves as a testament to the enduring fascination with pirates and their place in the collective imagination. Port Royal's infamous reputation is a captivating chapter in Jamaica's history, offering a glimpse into a tumultuous era that shaped the region's maritime heritage.

The Spanish Main: Treasure Hunting in the Caribbean

The Spanish Main, a term used to describe the mainland coast of the Spanish Empire in the Caribbean, holds a legendary status in the history of treasure hunting. This chapter explores the allure of the Spanish Main, the search for lost riches, and the enduring fascination with uncovering sunken treasure in the Caribbean's azure waters.

During the height of Spanish colonization in the 16th and 17th centuries, the Spanish Main was a hub of wealth and trade. The region encompassed vast territories, including present-day countries such as Colombia, Venezuela, Panama, and parts of Central America. Spain transported vast quantities of gold, silver, precious gemstones, and other valuable goods from its colonies back to Europe, fueling the Spanish Empire's power and wealth.

The allure of these riches, combined with the Caribbean's treacherous waters, unpredictable weather, and the vulnerability of Spanish galleons, led to a flourishing culture of piracy and privateering. Pirates and privateers targeted Spanish treasure ships, hoping to capture their valuable cargo and amass fortunes of their own.

The Caribbean became a playground for pirates, who roamed the seas in search of Spanish treasure. Infamous pirates, such as Sir Francis Drake and Henry Morgan, established their reputations by successfully raiding Spanish vessels and coastal settlements. These pirates would strike swiftly, utilizing their knowledge of the region's geography and the element of surprise to their advantage.

The Spanish Main's treacherous reputation was further enhanced by the presence of deadly reefs, strong currents, and unpredictable weather patterns. These natural hazards, combined with the need for precise navigation, made the waters around the Spanish Main perilous for seafarers. Ships carrying vast amounts of treasure were often lost to shipwrecks, further fueling the legends of sunken treasure waiting to be discovered.

The allure of treasure hunting in the Caribbean has captured the imagination of explorers, adventurers, and treasure seekers throughout history. Tales of hidden riches, lost cities, and sunken galleons have inspired countless expeditions and fueled the dreams of those hoping to uncover these elusive treasures.

The search for sunken treasure often involves the use of advanced technology and techniques. Underwater archaeologists and treasure hunters employ methods such as sonar scanning, metal detectors, and remotely operated vehicles (ROVs) to locate and recover artifacts from the ocean floor. These efforts seek not only to uncover valuable treasures but also to shed light on the historical and cultural significance of these underwater sites.

Numerous notable discoveries have been made in the search for treasure in the Caribbean. The wreck of the Spanish galleon Nuestra Señora de Atocha, which sank off the coast of Florida in 1622, yielded a wealth of gold, silver, and precious gemstones when it was discovered in the 1980s. Other famous shipwrecks, such as the Santa

Maria, the flagship of Christopher Columbus, have also captivated treasure hunters and historians alike.

Treasure hunting in the Caribbean, however, is not without controversy. The salvage of sunken treasure has raised ethical questions regarding ownership, cultural heritage, and the preservation of underwater archaeological sites. The delicate balance between the pursuit of valuable artifacts and the preservation of historical and cultural integrity is an ongoing challenge in the field of underwater archaeology.

The allure of the Spanish Main and the search for treasure in the Caribbean continue to captivate the human imagination. The tales of lost riches and sunken ships evoke a sense of adventure, discovery, and the possibilities of unearthing valuable historical artifacts. The pursuit of sunken treasure serves as a reminder of the region's complex history and the enduring fascination with the treasures that lie beneath the Caribbean's sparkling waters.

Treasure hunting in the Caribbean is a testament to the human desire to unravel the mysteries of the past, to connect with history, and to preserve the legacies of civilizations that have shaped the Caribbean's rich cultural tapestry. It is an ongoing exploration, seeking to uncover not just material wealth but also the stories, struggles, and triumphs of those who sailed the Spanish Main centuries ago.

The Maroons: Freedom Fighters of the Caribbean

The Maroons, a resilient and courageous group of people, emerged as freedom fighters in the Caribbean during the era of slavery. This chapter explores the history, struggles, and enduring legacies of the Maroons, highlighting their resistance against enslavement and their quest for freedom.

The Maroons were descendants of enslaved Africans who had escaped from plantations and established independent communities in the rugged and remote areas of the Caribbean islands. These communities provided sanctuary for those seeking liberation from the harsh conditions and brutality of plantation life. The term "Maroons" is derived from the Spanish word "cimarrón," which means "wild" or "untamed."

The origins of the Maroons can be traced back to various periods and regions of the Caribbean. In Jamaica, for example, the Maroons emerged as early as the mid-17th century, during the British colonization of the island. Other Caribbean islands, such as Dominica, Haiti, Suriname, and Guyana, also had significant Maroon populations.

Life as a Maroon was not easy. These communities had to adapt to the challenging and often hostile environments of the mountains, forests, and swamps where they sought refuge. They developed survival skills, such as hunting, farming, and herbal medicine, to sustain themselves in these remote regions.

The Maroons, fiercely committed to their freedom and the preservation of their cultural heritage, established organized societies with their own governance structures. They developed social, economic, and military systems that allowed them to defend their communities and resist recapture by slaveholders and colonial forces.

Maroon communities were often decentralized, with each group having its own leadership and governing structures. Chiefs or leaders, such as Cudjoe in Jamaica, Kojo in Suriname, and Mackandal in Haiti, emerged as key figures in the resistance against slavery. These leaders organized and coordinated attacks against plantations and engaged in guerrilla warfare tactics to defend their communities.

The Maroons employed a range of strategies in their resistance efforts. They utilized their knowledge of the local terrain to their advantage, launching surprise attacks and retreating to their inaccessible strongholds. They also established alliances with other marginalized groups, including indigenous populations and enslaved Africans, fostering a sense of solidarity in their struggle for freedom.

The success of the Maroons in resisting enslavement and establishing autonomous communities posed a significant challenge to the plantation economies and colonial powers. The British, French, and Dutch colonial authorities launched numerous military campaigns to suppress the Maroons, often resulting in prolonged conflicts. Treaties and agreements were sometimes negotiated, granting the Maroons limited autonomy and recognizing their rights to self-governance.

The legacies of the Maroons endure in the Caribbean to this day. Their resistance and determination inspired future generations in the fight against slavery and oppression. The stories and legends of Maroon leaders, their victories, and their strategies of resistance continue to be celebrated as part of the Caribbean's cultural heritage.

The Maroons also left a lasting impact on the region's cultural landscape. Their African traditions, music, dance, and spiritual practices have influenced Caribbean culture, particularly in countries like Jamaica and Suriname. Celebrations such as the Accompong Maroon Festival in Jamaica and the Grand Kadooment in Barbados pay homage to the Maroons' struggles and victories, reinforcing their importance in Caribbean history.

Recognizing the contributions of the Maroons is essential for understanding the complexities of Caribbean history and acknowledging the agency and resilience of those who fought for freedom. Their legacy serves as a reminder of the ongoing struggle for equality and justice in the Caribbean and beyond. The stories of the Maroons continue to inspire and empower individuals, highlighting the power of resistance and the quest for liberation in the face of adversity.

The Haitian Revolution: Birth of a Nation

The Haitian Revolution stands as a monumental event in history, marking the birth of the first independent black republic and the abolition of slavery in the Western Hemisphere. This chapter explores the complex and transformative journey of the Haitian Revolution, shedding light on its causes, key figures, revolutionary acts, and its profound impact on Haiti and the world.

The roots of the Haitian Revolution can be traced back to the harsh and brutal conditions of slavery in Saint-Domingue, the French colony that occupied the western part of the island of Hispaniola. By the late 18th century, Saint-Domingue had become the wealthiest colony in the Caribbean, largely due to its lucrative sugar, coffee, and indigo plantations that relied on the labor of enslaved Africans.

The enslaved population in Saint-Domingue vastly outnumbered the white planters and free population. This stark imbalance, coupled with the widespread mistreatment and oppression endured by the enslaved, created an environment ripe for resistance and rebellion. Additionally, the ideals of the French Revolution, with its emphasis on liberty, equality, and fraternity, inspired many in Saint-Domingue to question the legitimacy of slavery and the colonial order.

The Haitian Revolution began in August 1791 with a massive slave uprising in the north of Saint-Domingue. Led by figures such as Dutty Boukman, a Vodou priest, and Toussaint Louverture, a former slave who would become a prominent military leader, the rebels fought for their freedom and the abolition of slavery. The revolution quickly spread, engulfing the entire colony in a brutal and protracted conflict.

The revolutionaries faced formidable opposition from the French colonial forces, as well as other European powers that sought to suppress the rebellion. The British, Spanish, and even the United States became involved in the conflict, each with their own motivations and interests. The revolutionaries also had to contend with internal divisions and power struggles among their ranks.

Toussaint Louverture emerged as a central figure in the Haitian Revolution. His military prowess, strategic brilliance, and ability to navigate complex political dynamics allowed him to gain control over much of the island. Toussaint sought to forge a path of compromise with the French and secure the rights and freedom of the formerly enslaved population. However, his efforts were met with resistance from both the French and rival factions within Haiti.

By 1804, the revolutionaries, under the leadership of Jean-Jacques Dessalines following the capture and deportation of Toussaint Louverture, declared independence and established the Republic of Haiti. This monumental achievement made Haiti the first independent black republic in the world and dealt a severe blow to the institution of slavery.

The Haitian Revolution had far-reaching consequences. It shattered the myth of white supremacy and demonstrated the ability of enslaved Africans and their descendants to successfully overthrow colonial rule. The revolution sent shockwaves throughout the Atlantic world, inspiring enslaved populations elsewhere to challenge their oppressors and fight for freedom.

The success of the Haitian Revolution also had a profound impact on global geopolitics. It contributed to the decline of European colonialism in the Americas and influenced the course of subsequent anti-colonial movements around the world. The revolution's impact on the United States, particularly its impact on debates over slavery and racial equality, cannot be underestimated.

However, the Haitian Revolution also faced immense challenges and endured significant hardships. The newly formed republic faced isolation, economic embargoes, and political instability as it struggled to secure its place in the international community. External forces, such as France's demand for reparations in exchange for recognition of Haiti's independence, further hampered the young nation's development.

The legacy of the Haitian Revolution reverberates in Haiti's cultural identity and its ongoing struggle for social and economic justice. The revolutionaries' fight for freedom and equality continues to inspire Haitians to this day, reminding them of their resilience and the importance of self-determination.

The Haitian Revolution remains a testament to the indomitable human spirit, the quest for liberation, and the power of collective action. Its significance as a milestone in the history of both Haiti and the global struggle for human rights and equality cannot be overstated.

Cuba Libre: From Spanish Rule to Revolution

The story of Cuba's journey to independence is a complex and multifaceted one, marked by the struggles for self-determination, political upheaval, and social change. This chapter explores the path of Cuba from Spanish rule to revolution, delving into the historical events, key figures, and transformative moments that shaped the island's quest for freedom.

Cuba's history as a Spanish colony dates back to the arrival of Christopher Columbus in 1492. The island became an important outpost for Spanish colonization in the New World, serving as a strategic base for exploration, trade, and the exploitation of resources. Spanish settlers established plantations, primarily cultivating sugarcane, and relied on enslaved Africans for labor. Under Spanish rule, Cuba experienced cycles of economic prosperity and periods of unrest. The wealth generated by the sugar industry fueled the growth of cities such as Havana and Santiago de Cuba, attracting a diverse population of colonists, merchants, and enslaved Africans. However, the oppressive colonial system, along with restrictions on trade and political autonomy, created tensions and discontent among the Cuban population.

In the 19th century, waves of political and social change swept across Cuba. Inspired by Enlightenment ideals, movements advocating for political and economic reforms gained traction. The desire for greater autonomy and representation fueled the aspirations of Cuban nationalists who sought to break free from Spanish rule.

The Ten Years' War (1868-1878) marked a significant turning point in Cuba's struggle for independence. It was the first major armed conflict between Cuban rebels and Spanish colonial forces. Leaders such as Carlos Manuel de Céspedes and Ignacio Agramonte emerged as prominent figures in the fight for independence. The war, though ultimately unsuccessful in achieving complete independence, laid the groundwork for future uprisings and demonstrated the resilience of the Cuban people.

The Cuban independence movement gained momentum in the late 19th century with the emergence of the Cuban Revolutionary Party, led by José Martí. Martí, a writer and intellectual, became a symbol of Cuban nationalism and advocated for armed resistance against Spanish rule. His writings and speeches inspired a new generation of revolutionaries and galvanized support for the cause of Cuban independence. The Spanish-American War in 1898 proved to be a crucial moment in Cuba's path to independence. The conflict between the United States and Spain, sparked by the explosion of the USS Maine in Havana Harbor, resulted in the defeat of the Spanish forces and the end of Spanish colonial rule in Cuba. The United States assumed temporary control over the island, leading to a complex relationship between Cuba and its northern neighbor.

The early 20th century witnessed a struggle for political stability and self-governance in Cuba. The Platt Amendment, a provision inserted into the Cuban constitution by the United States, imposed certain limitations on Cuban sovereignty and granted the United States the right to intervene in Cuban affairs. This arrangement, coupled with political corruption and economic inequality, fueled discontent among the Cuban population. The desire for true independence and social justice found expression in the Cuban Revolution of 1959. Led by Fidel Castro, a young lawyer and revolutionary, the revolution aimed to overthrow the authoritarian regime of Fulgencio Batista and establish a socialist government. The revolutionaries, including Che Guevara, fought a guerrilla war from the mountains of Sierra Maestra, gaining popular support and ultimately toppling the Batista regime.

The Cuban Revolution brought sweeping social and economic changes to the island. The nationalization of industries, agrarian reforms, and the establishment of a centrally planned economy transformed Cuba's socioeconomic landscape. The revolution also marked a shift in Cuba's foreign relations, with the country aligning itself with the Soviet Union and adopting socialist policies.

The Cuban Revolution's impact has been the subject of ongoing debate and interpretation. Supporters laud its achievements in education, healthcare, and social equality, while critics point to restrictions on political freedoms and human rights. The revolution's global significance as a symbol of anti-imperialism and resistance to Western dominance cannot be denied.

Cuba's journey from Spanish rule to revolution is a testament to the perseverance and determination of its people in the pursuit of independence and self-determination. The island's history, marked by colonialism, struggle, and transformation, continues to shape its identity and its place in the world.

Puerto Rico: A Tale of Colonization and Identity

Puerto Rico, an island in the Caribbean, carries a complex history of colonization and a distinct cultural identity. This chapter explores the narrative of Puerto Rico, tracing the impacts of colonization, the struggles for autonomy, and the ongoing quest for a defined political status and sense of identity.

The colonization of Puerto Rico began in 1493 when Christopher Columbus arrived during his second voyage to the Americas. The island became a Spanish possession and was initially used as a military outpost and a stopover point for Spanish expeditions in the region. Spanish settlers established agricultural plantations, primarily cultivating sugarcane, and brought enslaved Africans to work on the island.

Under Spanish rule, Puerto Rico experienced economic growth and cultural influence. The Spanish colonial government established cities, such as San Juan, and implemented governance systems that shaped the island's social structure. The Spanish language, Catholicism, and European traditions became deeply ingrained in Puerto Rican society.

The 19th century brought significant changes to Puerto Rico's political landscape. In 1898, following the Spanish-American War, Puerto Rico became a territory of the United States as part of the Treaty of Paris. The transition from Spanish to American rule marked a period of profound transformation and uncertainty for the island and its inhabitants.

Throughout the 20th century, Puerto Rico's political status remained a subject of debate and contention. The island was granted limited self-governance in 1952, becoming a Commonwealth of the United States. This arrangement allowed Puerto Rico to have its own local government, but ultimate decision-making authority still rested with the U.S. federal government.

The question of Puerto Rico's political status continues to be a central issue for the island. The three main options often discussed are statehood, independence, or maintaining the current Commonwealth status. These options have sparked passionate debates and have shaped Puerto Rico's political landscape.

The cultural identity of Puerto Rico reflects a blend of indigenous, Spanish, African, and American influences. Puerto Ricans embrace their unique heritage, celebrating their Afro-Caribbean roots, Taino indigenous ancestry, and Spanish traditions. The island's music, such as salsa, bomba, and reggaeton, is renowned worldwide and serves as a vibrant expression of Puerto Rican identity.

Puerto Rico's relationship with the United States has had significant economic implications. The island has benefited from certain economic advantages, such as tax incentives and access to the U.S. market. However, it has also faced challenges, including economic dependency, high levels of poverty, and limited representation in U.S. federal institutions.

Natural disasters, such as hurricanes and earthquakes, have further complicated Puerto Rico's path to economic stability and political self-determination. These events have exposed vulnerabilities and highlighted the need for robust infrastructure, disaster preparedness, and resilient recovery efforts.

Puerto Rico's quest for a defined political status and identity remains an ongoing struggle. The island's population is diverse in its opinions and aspirations, with different factions advocating for various paths forward. Achieving consensus on the island's political future and identity is a complex endeavor, requiring careful consideration of historical, cultural, economic, and political factors.

The story of Puerto Rico is a tale of colonization, resilience, and cultural richness. It is a testament to the enduring spirit of its people, who navigate the complexities of their history while forging a path towards a future that reflects their collective aspirations and desires for self-determination. The search for a clear political status and a strong sense of identity continues to shape the narrative of Puerto Rico and its place in the Caribbean and the world.

The Lesser Antilles: Gems of the Caribbean

The Lesser Antilles, a stunning chain of islands in the Caribbean Sea, captivate with their natural beauty, vibrant cultures, and rich histories. This chapter explores the enchanting allure of the Lesser Antilles, delving into their geographical diversity, cultural tapestry, and the unique experiences they offer to visitors.

The Lesser Antilles stretch southeast from the Virgin Islands to Trinidad and Tobago, forming a bridge between the Greater Antilles and South America. This archipelago is divided into two groups: the Leeward Islands to the north, and the Windward Islands to the south. Each island possesses its own distinct character and charm, making the region a treasure trove for exploration.

The islands of the Lesser Antilles exhibit remarkable geographical diversity. From the volcanic peaks of Dominica and St. Lucia to the flat coral atolls of the Grenadines, each island showcases a unique topography shaped by millions of years of geological activity. These diverse landscapes offer breathtaking vistas, lush rainforests, cascading waterfalls, and pristine beaches that enchant travelers from around the world.

The Lesser Antilles are home to a tapestry of cultures that reflect the historical influences of various European powers, indigenous peoples, and African heritage. The islands were colonized by different European nations, including the British, French, Dutch, and Spanish, resulting in a blend of European and Afro-Caribbean traditions. The rich cultural heritage is evident in the local cuisine, music, dance, and festivals that infuse each island with its own vibrant character.

The islands of the Lesser Antilles are renowned for their vibrant and diverse marine ecosystems. The crystal-clear waters surrounding the islands teem with colorful coral reefs, tropical fish, and other marine life, making them ideal destinations for snorkeling and diving enthusiasts. The region's warm and inviting waters also provide opportunities for water sports, including sailing, windsurfing, and kitesurfing.

Each island in the Lesser Antilles boasts its own unique attractions and landmarks. Barbados entices visitors with its stunning beaches, colonial architecture, and vibrant nightlife. St. Kitts and Nevis offer a glimpse into the colonial past with their well-preserved plantation houses and historic sites. Antigua and Barbuda boast some of the Caribbean's most beautiful beaches and offer opportunities for exploring secluded coves and offshore reefs.

Grenada, known as the "Spice Isle," captivates with its aromatic nutmeg and cocoa plantations, as well as its stunning waterfalls and rainforests. The island of St. Vincent showcases its dramatic volcanic landscapes, including the iconic La Soufrière volcano. Dominica, the "Nature Island," enthralls with its untouched rainforests, hot springs, and hiking trails that lead to hidden waterfalls and breathtaking viewpoints.

The islands of Martinique and Guadeloupe, both overseas territories of France, combine Caribbean charm with a distinct French influence. Visitors can explore the colonial architecture, indulge in French cuisine, and soak up the unique blend of cultures that define these islands.

The pristine beauty and warm hospitality of the Lesser Antilles make them an ideal destination for nature lovers, adventure seekers, and those in search of tranquility. Whether it's hiking through lush rainforests, lounging on picturesque beaches, or immersing oneself in the vibrant local cultures, the Lesser Antilles offer a wealth of experiences that cater to diverse interests.

While tourism plays a significant role in the economies of many Lesser Antilles islands, it is important to strike a balance between development and environmental preservation. Sustainable tourism practices, such as protected marine areas and responsible land management, are crucial for maintaining the natural beauty and ecological integrity of the islands.

The Lesser Antilles, with their breathtaking landscapes, vibrant cultures, and rich histories, are indeed gems of the Caribbean. Their diverse offerings provide a tapestry of experiences that leave indelible memories for those fortunate enough to explore their shores. Whether it's the idyllic beaches, lush rainforests, or the warmth of the local communities, the Lesser Antilles continue to captivate visitors and stand as shining gems in the Caribbean Sea.

Jamaica: Reggae, Rum, and Rastafarianism

Jamaica, an island jewel in the Caribbean Sea, is known worldwide for its vibrant culture, rhythmic music, and unique religious movement. This chapter explores the multifaceted aspects of Jamaica, diving into its iconic music genre, the rich tradition of rum, and the philosophy of Rastafarianism that has left an indelible mark on the island's identity.

Reggae, a musical genre that originated in Jamaica, has become synonymous with the island's cultural expression. With its infectious rhythms, soulful melodies, and powerful messages, reggae music has resonated with people across the globe. The genre gained international recognition through the legendary Bob Marley, who became an icon for his powerful lyrics and dedication to social justice. Reggae's themes of love, unity, and political consciousness continue to inspire artists and uplift audiences worldwide. Jamaica's musical heritage extends beyond reggae. The island is also renowned for other genres such as ska, rocksteady, and dancehall. Each genre carries its own unique characteristics and has played a significant role in shaping Jamaica's musical landscape. These genres serve as a reflection of the island's cultural diversity, creativity, and the resilience of its people.

Rum, with its deep historical roots, is an integral part of Jamaica's cultural fabric. The island's fertile land and ideal climate provide the perfect conditions for sugarcane cultivation, the key ingredient in rum production.

Jamaica's rum distilleries, some with centuries-old traditions, produce a wide range of rums that are enjoyed both locally and internationally. From the smooth sipping rums to the potent overproof varieties, Jamaica's rum industry has become a source of national pride.

Rastafarianism, a religious and social movement that emerged in Jamaica in the early 20th century, has had a profound impact on the island's cultural and spiritual landscape. The movement's roots can be traced back to the teachings of Marcus Garvey, a Jamaican activist who advocated for the empowerment and unity of black people worldwide. Rastafarians embrace a belief in the divinity of Emperor Haile Selassie I of Ethiopia and adhere to a way of life that promotes equality, peace, and a connection with nature.

The iconic symbols of Rastafarianism, such as the dreadlocks hairstyle, vibrant colors, and the prominent use of cannabis as a sacrament, have become synonymous with Jamaica's cultural identity. Rastafarianism's influence extends beyond religious practice and permeates various aspects of Jamaican society, including art, music, fashion, and social activism. The movement's emphasis on social justice and its call for the upliftment of marginalized communities have made a lasting impact on Jamaica and the world.

Jamaica's cultural heritage is a tapestry woven with diverse influences, including the indigenous Taino people, the colonial legacies of the Spanish and British, and the cultural contributions of African slaves. This fusion of influences has given rise to a vibrant and dynamic society that celebrates its roots while embracing innovation and change.

The beauty of Jamaica's natural environment adds to its allure. The island's stunning beaches, lush mountains, and vibrant flora and fauna attract visitors from around the globe. The Blue Mountains, home to the world-famous Jamaican Blue Mountain coffee, offer breathtaking vistas and opportunities for hiking and exploration. The cascading waterfalls, such as Dunn's River Falls and YS Falls, provide refreshing escapes and showcase the island's natural wonders.

Jamaica's tourism industry has played a significant role in its economic development. Visitors flock to the island to experience its warm hospitality, vibrant culture, and breathtaking landscapes. Tourism has created employment opportunities and contributed to infrastructure development, while also presenting challenges related to environmental sustainability and maintaining a balance between economic growth and cultural preservation.

Jamaica's journey as a nation has been shaped by its music, its rich cultural traditions, and the spiritual philosophy of Rastafarianism. The island's contributions to the world extend beyond its physical boundaries, inspiring people through music, spreading cultural awareness, and promoting a message of unity and social justice.

As Jamaica continues to evolve, its unique blend of reggae, rum, and Rastafarianism remains an integral part of its national identity and global reputation. The island's cultural riches, warm spirit, and captivating landscapes make it a place of enduring fascination and an experience that lingers long after one's departure.

Trinidad and Tobago: Carnival and Cultural Fusion

Trinidad and Tobago, a dynamic twin-island nation in the southern Caribbean, is renowned for its vibrant Carnival celebrations and rich cultural heritage. This chapter explores the captivating fusion of cultures found in Trinidad and Tobago, delving into the origins of Carnival, the diverse ethnic influences, and the island's enduring commitment to artistic expression.

Carnival, the most anticipated and celebrated event in Trinidad and Tobago, is a dazzling spectacle of music, dance, and colorful costumes. The origins of Carnival can be traced back to the colonial era when enslaved Africans and indentured laborers from India, as well as other immigrant communities, used the festival as a form of cultural expression and liberation.

Today, Trinidad and Tobago's Carnival is a magnificent display of creativity and joy. Calypso and soca music, with their infectious rhythms and clever lyrics, set the stage for revelers to dance through the streets in elaborate costumes. The steelpan, the national instrument of Trinidad and Tobago, also takes center stage, with vibrant steel orchestras showcasing their musical prowess during the festivities. Carnival in Trinidad and Tobago is a melting pot of cultures, reflecting the island's diverse heritage. The African influence is evident in the energetic drumming, traditional masquerade characters like the Moko Jumbie and the Dame Lorraine, and the pulsating rhythms of calypso music. Indian traditions are celebrated through the melodic sounds of the sitar, the rhythmic beats of the dholak, and the graceful movements of traditional Indian dance forms, such as chutney and Bollywood-inspired dances.

Other cultural influences, including Chinese, European, and Middle Eastern, contribute to the vibrant tapestry of Trinidad and Tobago's Carnival. The Chinese community showcases its rich heritage through the dazzling spectacle of dragon dances and vibrant displays of traditional attire. European influences are evident in the elegant ballroom dances and the masquerade traditions that hark back to the colonial era. The Middle Eastern community adds its own flair with the vibrant rhythms of tassa drumming and the intricate art of belly dancing.

Beyond Carnival, Trinidad and Tobago's cultural fusion is evident in its everyday life. The islands' population is composed of people from diverse ethnic backgrounds, including Afro-Trinidadians, Indo-Trinidadians, Chinese-Trinidadians, Syrian-Trinidadians, and others. This cultural diversity has shaped the island's traditions, languages, cuisine, and artistic expressions, fostering a sense of unity and respect for different cultures.

Trinidad and Tobago's commitment to artistic expression extends beyond Carnival. The islands are known for their vibrant arts scene, with local artists excelling in various disciplines, including visual arts, literature, theater, and film. The country has produced internationally acclaimed authors, such as V.S. Naipaul and Earl Lovelace, who have garnered global recognition for their literary contributions. Music remains an integral part of Trinidad and Tobago's cultural landscape beyond Carnival. The islands have given birth to numerous musical genres, including calypso, soca, steelpan, and chutney. These genres have not only gained popularity locally but have also made a significant impact on the global music scene, influencing artists and audiences worldwide.

Trinidad and Tobago's commitment to cultural preservation and celebration is evident in its numerous festivals and events throughout the year. These include Divali, a Hindu festival of lights; Eid-ul-Fitr, marking the end of Ramadan; and Hosay, a Shia Muslim commemoration. These festivals further showcase the country's cultural diversity and provide opportunities for communities to come together in celebration.

The natural beauty of Trinidad and Tobago also adds to their allure. From the lush rainforests and stunning waterfalls of Trinidad to the pristine beaches and coral reefs of Tobago, the islands offer a wealth of natural wonders for exploration and relaxation.

Trinidad and Tobago's commitment to cultural fusion, artistic expression, and celebration of diversity has fostered a sense of national identity that transcends ethnic boundaries. The islands continue to embrace their multicultural heritage and serve as a testament to the power of cultural exchange and the beauty of unity in diversity.

As Trinidad and Tobago's Carnival and cultural traditions evolve, they remain vibrant symbols of the nation's spirit, creativity, and commitment to celebrating its rich heritage. The islands' fusion of cultures serves as an inspiration and a reminder of the beauty that emerges when people come together to celebrate their shared humanity.

Barbados: Sun, Sand, and British Heritage

Barbados, a gem of the Caribbean, is renowned for its pristine beaches, warm hospitality, and rich British heritage. This chapter delves into the allure of Barbados, exploring its idyllic natural landscapes, colonial history, and the enduring influence of its British roots.

Situated in the eastern Caribbean, Barbados boasts stunning coastlines adorned with powdery white sands and crystal-clear turquoise waters. The island's natural beauty is accentuated by its coral reefs, lush gardens, and rolling hills. From the iconic Crane Beach to the serene waters of Carlisle Bay, Barbados offers an array of breathtaking locations for sunbathing, swimming, and water sports.

The history of Barbados is deeply intertwined with its colonial past. The island was first settled by the English in 1627, making it one of the earliest British colonies in the Caribbean. British influence shaped the island's social, political, and economic landscape for centuries to come.

Barbados became a major producer of sugar during the colonial era, and the plantations that once dominated the island's interior stand as a testament to this history. The plantation system relied heavily on the labor of enslaved Africans, who were brought to the island to work on the sugar estates. The legacy of slavery and the plantation system continues to shape Barbados' cultural fabric and collective memory.

The British influence on Barbados is evident in its governance, legal system, education, and cultural traditions. The island follows the Westminster system of government, with a parliamentary democracy modeled after the British system. The English common law forms the basis of the island's legal framework. The educational system reflects British traditions, with an emphasis on academic excellence and a curriculum that incorporates subjects such as English literature and history.

Barbados' British heritage is also visible in its architecture. Historic buildings, such as the Parliament Buildings in Bridgetown and St. Nicholas Abbey, showcase the island's colonial past. The Anglican Church, with its beautiful churches and cathedrals, reflects the influence of the Church of England.

Despite its British ties, Barbados has developed its unique cultural identity. The island's vibrant music, such as calypso, soca, and the indigenous tuk band, reflects the spirit and creativity of its people. The Bajan dialect, a distinct blend of English and African languages, adds to the island's linguistic charm.

Barbados' culinary scene is a fusion of British, African, and West Indian flavors. Bajan cuisine features dishes such as flying fish, cou-cou, macaroni pie, and pudding and souse. The island's rum industry, dating back to the colonial era, produces some of the finest rums in the world, adding to the island's gastronomic delights.

Barbados' relationship with Britain remains strong, as it maintains ties as a member of the Commonwealth and recognizes Queen Elizabeth II as the ceremonial head of state. The British influence can be seen in events such as the changing of the sentry at the Garrison Savannah and the celebration of important British holidays like Boxing Day.

Barbados' cultural identity extends beyond its British heritage. The island celebrates its African roots through events such as the Crop Over festival, a vibrant extravaganza of music, dance, and revelry that marks the end of the sugarcane harvest. The festival showcases the island's rich cultural traditions and serves as a testament to its resilience and joie de vivre.

Barbados has also made significant strides towards independence and self-governance. The island achieved independence from Britain on November 30, 1966, while maintaining a strong bond with the British Commonwealth. This independence has allowed Barbados to develop its own unique path and forge its place in the global community.

Barbados' natural beauty, warm hospitality, and British heritage combine to create a captivating destination that entices visitors from around the world. Whether it's exploring historic sites, basking on sun-drenched beaches, or immersing oneself in the island's vibrant culture, Barbados offers a wealth of experiences that embody the essence of Caribbean charm intertwined with its enduring British heritage.

The Dominican Republic: Merengue and Dominicanidad

The Dominican Republic, a vibrant country in the Caribbean, is renowned for its lively music, rich cultural heritage, and a strong sense of national identity known as Dominicanidad. This chapter explores the captivating rhythms of merengue, the diverse cultural influences that shape Dominicanidad, and the country's unique blend of traditions.

Merengue, the national music and dance of the Dominican Republic, is a pulsating and infectious genre that reflects the spirit and joy of the Dominican people. Its lively beat, characterized by the rhythmic combination of the güira, tambora, and accordion, creates an irresistible urge to dance. Merengue is an integral part of Dominican social gatherings, festivals, and celebrations, serving as a vibrant expression of national pride and cultural unity.

The roots of merengue can be traced back to the mid-19th century, originating in the rural areas of the Dominican Republic. Influenced by African, European, and indigenous Taino musical traditions, merengue evolved into a distinctive genre that showcases the country's cultural diversity. Over the years, merengue has gained international recognition, captivating audiences around the world with its infectious rhythms and lively melodies.

Dominicanidad, or the Dominican identity, is deeply ingrained in the country's cultural fabric. It encompasses a strong sense of national pride, an appreciation for the country's history and traditions, and a recognition of the diverse influences that have shaped Dominican culture. Dominicanidad celebrates the fusion of African, European, and indigenous Taino heritage, highlighting the country's unique cultural tapestry.

The Dominican Republic's history is intertwined with a complex legacy of colonization, slavery, and independence. The island of Hispaniola, where the Dominican Republic is located, was the site of Christopher Columbus' first landing in the Americas in 1492. It subsequently became a Spanish colony, and the legacy of Spanish colonization is still evident in the country's language, religion (predominantly Catholicism), and architectural heritage.

The African influence in the Dominican Republic is a significant component of Dominicanidad. During the era of slavery, African captives were brought to the island to work on sugar plantations, contributing to the cultural diversity and rich Afro-Dominican traditions. African rhythms, dances, and religious practices have permeated Dominican music and culture, adding depth and vibrancy to the country's artistic expressions.

The indigenous Taino heritage, although diminished after the arrival of European colonizers, continues to shape Dominican identity. The Taino people were the original inhabitants of Hispaniola and made significant contributions to the island's culture, language, and agriculture. Today, efforts are being made to preserve and celebrate Taino traditions and artifacts, providing a deeper understanding of the country's indigenous roots.

Spanish colonial architecture can be seen throughout the Dominican Republic, particularly in the historic city of Santo Domingo, which boasts the first cathedral, hospital, and university in the New World. The Zona Colonial, a UNESCO World Heritage Site, offers a glimpse into the country's colonial past with its cobblestone streets, grand plazas, and well-preserved buildings.

The Dominican Republic's natural beauty is equally captivating. From the stunning beaches of Punta Cana and Puerto Plata to the lush mountains of Jarabacoa and Constanza, the country offers diverse landscapes that attract nature lovers and adventure seekers. The Caribbean Sea, with its turquoise waters, coral reefs, and abundant marine life, provides opportunities for snorkeling, scuba diving, and water sports.

Culinary delights play a significant role in Dominican culture. The country's cuisine is a fusion of Spanish, African, and Taino flavors, featuring dishes such as sancocho (a hearty stew), mofongo (a mashed plantain dish), and tostones (fried plantains). The Dominican Republic is also known for its world-class cigars and rum, both of which have gained international acclaim.

The Dominican Republic's commitment to arts and literature is evident in the vibrant cultural scene. The country has produced renowned writers, musicians, and visual artists who have made significant contributions to their respective fields. Festivals and cultural events, such as the Dominican Carnival and the Festival de Merengue, showcase the country's artistic talents and serve as vibrant celebrations of Dominicanidad.

The Dominican Republic's rich cultural heritage, merengue rhythms, and Dominicanidad provide a fascinating glimpse into the country's soul and identity. The fusion of African, European, and indigenous influences creates a dynamic and captivating culture that continues to evolve while honoring its roots. The spirit of the Dominican people, the vibrancy of their traditions, and the passion for life serve as a testament to the enduring allure of the Dominican Republic.

The Bahamas: Paradise Islands and Underwater Wonders

The Bahamas, an archipelago of stunning islands in the Atlantic Ocean, is synonymous with paradise. This chapter explores the allure of the Bahamas, from its breathtaking islands and pristine beaches to the captivating underwater world that lies beneath its turquoise waters.

The Bahamas is composed of more than 700 islands and cays, each offering its own unique charm and beauty. Among the most renowned islands are Nassau, the capital city, and Freeport, the second-largest city, both bustling with vibrant culture and entertainment. Other popular destinations include Paradise Island, known for its luxurious resorts and the iconic Atlantis Paradise Island, and the Exumas, a pristine chain of islands renowned for their untouched natural beauty.

The beaches of the Bahamas are truly idyllic, with their powdery white sands and crystal-clear waters. From the famous Cable Beach in Nassau to the secluded shores of Harbour Island, the Bahamas boasts an array of stunning coastal landscapes that invite relaxation, water sports, and sun-soaked adventures. Whether it's swimming, snorkeling, or simply basking in the sun, the beaches of the Bahamas offer a paradise-like experience.

One of the Bahamas' most treasured attractions is its remarkable underwater world. The crystal-clear waters and extensive coral reef systems make it a diver's and snorkeler's paradise. The Andros Barrier Reef, the third-largest barrier reef in the world, is a haven for marine life and offers breathtaking underwater vistas. The Bahamas is also home to the famous Blue Hole, a natural wonder that attracts divers from around the world with its deep vertical caves and awe-inspiring formations.

The marine biodiversity of the Bahamas is exceptional, with an abundance of colorful fish, sea turtles, dolphins, and even the occasional encounter with majestic creatures like sharks and rays. The Exumas' famous swimming pigs and the opportunity to swim with nurse sharks at Compass Cay are unique experiences that add to the allure of the Bahamas.

Beyond its natural wonders, the Bahamas boasts a rich cultural heritage. The islands have been shaped by the influences of various European powers, including the British, Spanish, and French. The British colonial influence is particularly prominent, as the Bahamas remained a British colony until gaining independence in 1973. The remnants of British colonial architecture, such as the Government House in Nassau, reflect this heritage.

The Bahamian people are known for their warm hospitality and vibrant culture. The Junkanoo festival, a colorful and energetic street parade, is one of the most celebrated cultural events in the Bahamas. It showcases Bahamian music, dance, and artistry, with participants adorned in vibrant costumes and elaborate headdresses.

The cuisine of the Bahamas is a delightful blend of flavors influenced by African, British, and Caribbean traditions. Seafood, including conch (a local delicacy), grouper, and lobster, features prominently in Bahamian dishes. Traditional dishes like conch fritters, peas and rice, and guava duff provide a delicious taste of the local culinary scene.

Tourism plays a significant role in the Bahamian economy, with visitors drawn to the islands' natural beauty, warm climate, and welcoming atmosphere. The tourism industry has led to the development of world-class resorts, luxury accommodations, and a wide range of recreational activities and entertainment options.

Preserving the natural environment is a priority in the Bahamas, as the government and local communities recognize the importance of sustainable tourism and protecting the delicate ecosystems. Efforts are made to maintain the integrity of the coral reefs, protect endangered species, and promote responsible eco-tourism practices.

The Bahamas truly lives up to its reputation as a paradise destination, offering a captivating blend of paradise islands, breathtaking beaches, and underwater wonders. From the vibrant culture and warm hospitality of its people to the natural beauty and biodiversity of its marine life, the Bahamas provides a truly unforgettable experience for travelers seeking a tropical haven.

Grenada: The Spice Isle of the Caribbean

Grenada, known as the Spice Isle of the Caribbean, is a captivating island nation that offers a rich cultural heritage, stunning natural beauty, and a long-standing reputation as a major producer of spices. This chapter delves into the allure of Grenada, exploring its fragrant spice industry, diverse ecosystems, and the warmth of its people.

Grenada's moniker, the Spice Isle, is well-deserved. The island's fertile soil and tropical climate provide the ideal conditions for cultivating a wide range of spices. Nutmeg, the most iconic spice associated with Grenada, takes center stage. Known as the "Jewel of the Caribbean," Grenada is one of the world's largest producers of nutmeg, accounting for a significant portion of global supply. The scent of nutmeg fills the air, and the spice is a prominent ingredient in Grenadian cuisine, beverages, and even local crafts.

Beyond nutmeg, Grenada's spice industry also includes cloves, cinnamon, ginger, and turmeric, among others. The cultivation of these aromatic spices has been a mainstay of Grenada's economy for centuries, with the spice trade bringing prosperity to the island. Spice plantations, such as the Belmont Estate and the Dougaldston Spice Estate, offer visitors a glimpse into Grenada's spice heritage, with guided tours and interactive experiences that showcase the process of harvesting and processing these fragrant treasures.

Grenada's natural beauty extends far beyond its spice plantations. The island's lush rainforests, pristine beaches, and stunning waterfalls captivate visitors from around the world. Grand Etang National Park, located in the island's mountainous interior, is a haven for nature lovers, with its diverse flora and fauna, hiking trails, and the breathtaking Grand Etang Lake. Annandale Falls, Concord Falls, and Seven Sisters Falls are among the many cascading waterfalls that add to Grenada's natural charm.

The coastline of Grenada is dotted with picturesque beaches, each offering its own unique appeal. Grand Anse Beach, with its powdery white sand and azure waters, is often ranked among the best beaches in the Caribbean. La Sagesse Beach, Morne Rouge Beach, and Levera Beach are also popular choices, providing opportunities for swimming, snorkeling, and simply basking in the sun.

Grenada's culture is a vibrant tapestry woven with influences from African, European, and indigenous Carib and Arawak peoples. The island's official language is English, reflecting its historical ties to British colonization. The warmth and friendliness of the Grenadian people are evident in their hospitality, vibrant festivals, and lively music.

Music plays a central role in Grenadian culture, with genres such as calypso, soca, and reggae dominating the airwaves. The annual Grenada Carnival, known as Spicemas, is a colorful extravaganza of music, dance, and revelry that showcases the island's vibrant cultural expressions. Steelpan music, with its rhythmic melodies and vibrant steel orchestras, adds a distinct Caribbean flavor to the musical landscape.

Grenadian cuisine is a delightful fusion of flavors and influences. The island's culinary scene reflects its rich cultural heritage, with dishes that blend African, European, and indigenous traditions. Seafood is a staple, with fresh fish, lobster, and shrimp featuring prominently in Grenadian recipes. Popular dishes include oil down, a flavorful one-pot meal made with coconut milk, breadfruit, and a variety of meats and vegetables. Grenada's street food scene also delights with local favorites like roti, a savory wrap filled with curried meat or vegetables.

Grenada's commitment to environmental sustainability is evident in its efforts to protect its natural resources and promote eco-tourism. The island is home to the world's first underwater sculpture park, a unique artistic installation that doubles as an artificial reef, providing habitats for marine life and attracting snorkelers and divers.

Grenada's economy relies not only on spices but also on tourism, agriculture, and a developing offshore finance sector. The country's commitment to sustainable development and the preservation of its natural and cultural heritage serves as a testament to its long-term vision.

Grenada, with its intoxicating aromas, stunning landscapes, and warm-hearted people, offers a glimpse into the authentic spirit of the Caribbean. The Spice Isle continues to captivate visitors with its diverse offerings, inviting them to savor the flavors, explore the natural wonders, and embrace the vibrant culture that make Grenada a true gem of the Caribbean.

Curaçao: A Dutch Caribbean Jewel

Curaçao, a captivating island nestled in the Dutch Caribbean, offers a unique blend of European charm, vibrant culture, and stunning natural beauty. This chapter explores the allure of Curaçao, from its rich history as a Dutch colony to its picturesque landscapes and diverse cultural heritage.

Curaçao's history dates back to the early 17th century when the island was colonized by the Dutch. As part of the Netherlands Antilles until its dissolution in 2010, Curaçao remains an autonomous country within the Kingdom of the Netherlands. The island's Dutch colonial past is evident in its architecture, language, and governance.

The colorful capital city of Willemstad is a UNESCO World Heritage site and a testament to Curaçao's Dutch influence. The iconic pastel-colored buildings that line the streets of Punda and Otrobanda reflect the island's colonial heritage. The distinctive Dutch gables, quaint courtyards, and charming narrow alleyways create an atmosphere reminiscent of a European village.

Language is another aspect that showcases the Dutch influence in Curaçao. While Papiamentu, a Creole language derived from Portuguese, Spanish, Dutch, and African languages, is widely spoken, Dutch is the official language of the island. English and Spanish are also commonly understood and spoken, making Curaçao a linguistically diverse destination.

Curaçao's cultural heritage is a vibrant tapestry woven with influences from Africa, Europe, and the Americas. The island's population is a diverse mix of Afro-Curaçaoans, Dutch descendants, and immigrants from neighboring Caribbean islands, Latin America, and beyond. This cultural fusion is reflected in the island's music, cuisine, and traditions.

Music plays an integral role in Curaçao's cultural landscape. The island is known for its unique musical genre, Tumba, characterized by its energetic rhythms and captivating melodies. During the annual Carnival celebrations, Tumba takes center stage, with lively parades, vibrant costumes, and pulsating music filling the streets of Willemstad.

Curaçao's culinary scene is a delightful fusion of flavors and influences. The island's cuisine combines Dutch, African, and Latin American elements, creating a diverse array of dishes that tantalize the taste buds. Local specialties include Keshi Yena, a savory dish made with Gouda cheese and filled with flavorful meat, and Stobá, a slow-cooked meat or vegetable stew. Seafood, such as fresh fish and shrimp, features prominently in Curaçaoan cuisine.

The natural beauty of Curaçao is equally captivating. Pristine beaches with turquoise waters, such as Cas Abao Beach and Playa Kenepa, offer idyllic spots for swimming, snorkeling, and sunbathing. The island's underwater world is a paradise for divers, with vibrant coral reefs teeming with marine life, including colorful fish, sea turtles, and even the occasional sighting of dolphins and eagle rays.

Curaçao's commitment to environmental preservation is evident in its marine parks and protected areas. The Curaçao Sea Aquarium and the Curaçao Underwater Marine Park offer opportunities to explore the diverse marine ecosystems while promoting sustainable practices and conservation efforts.

The island's cultural heritage is celebrated through events such as the Curaçao North Sea Jazz Festival, which attracts world-renowned musicians and showcases a fusion of international and local talent. The annual Curaçao Carnival is a highlight of the island's cultural calendar, with vibrant parades, festive music, and traditional dances.

Curaçao's economic prosperity relies on a combination of industries, including tourism, oil refining, and international finance. The island's favorable tax policies and stable financial system have positioned it as a hub for international business and offshore banking.

Curaçao's warm climate, rich history, and natural beauty make it an enchanting destination in the Dutch Caribbean. The island's unique blend of European and Caribbean influences, coupled with its welcoming ambiance, offers visitors a truly unforgettable experience. From exploring the colorful streets of Willemstad to immersing oneself in the underwater wonders, Curaçao shines as a jewel in the Caribbean crown.

St. Kitts and Nevis: The First British Colony in the Caribbean

St. Kitts and Nevis, a picturesque duo of islands nestled in the Caribbean Sea, hold the distinction of being the first British colony in the Caribbean. This chapter explores the rich history, natural beauty, and cultural heritage of St. Kitts and Nevis, painting a vivid picture of their significance in the region.

The story of St. Kitts and Nevis begins with the arrival of European explorers in the late 15th century. Christopher Columbus is believed to have sighted the islands during his second voyage in 1493, naming them after Saint Christopher (St. Kitts) and Nevis, a reference to the Spanish word for snow.

In the early 17th century, the British established their presence on St. Kitts, making it the first permanent British settlement in the Caribbean. The island became a major center of sugar production, fueled by the labor of enslaved Africans. The British colonial influence shaped the islands' society, culture, and economy for centuries to come.

The strategic location of St. Kitts and Nevis in the Caribbean made them attractive to European powers seeking to establish control in the region. Over the years, the islands changed hands between the British and the French multiple times, with each colonial power leaving its mark on the islands' history and architecture.

The legacy of the sugar plantation era is evident in the remnants of the once-thriving industry that dot the landscape. The imposing Brimstone Hill Fortress National Park, a UNESCO World Heritage site, stands as a testament to the island's turbulent past and serves as a reminder of the strategic importance of St. Kitts.

St. Kitts and Nevis offer a wealth of natural beauty. The islands are blessed with lush tropical landscapes, pristine beaches, and volcanic peaks. The dormant volcano, Mount Liamuiga, on St. Kitts, is a popular hiking destination, offering breathtaking panoramic views from its summit. Nevis, with its tranquil charm and idyllic beaches, provides a serene escape for visitors seeking relaxation and seclusion.

The Kittitian and Nevisian people, known as Kittitians and Nevisians, respectively, reflect the islands' rich cultural heritage. The majority of the population is of African descent, with additional influences from European, indigenous Carib, and East Indian communities. The fusion of these cultures is celebrated through vibrant festivals, music, and cuisine.

Music plays a central role in Kittitian and Nevisian culture. The islands are known for their lively musical genres, including soca, calypso, and reggae. Local artists, such as the legendary soca artist Arrow, have achieved international acclaim, spreading the vibrant sounds of the islands across the globe.

The culinary scene of St. Kitts and Nevis showcases a blend of African, European, and Caribbean flavors. Local dishes like goat water (a hearty meat stew), saltfish and johnnycake, and conch fritters tantalize the taste buds with their unique blend of spices and ingredients.

Today, St. Kitts and Nevis are independent countries within the Commonwealth, with a parliamentary democracy based on the British system. The islands continue to attract visitors with their natural beauty, historical landmarks, and warm hospitality. The tourism industry, along with agriculture and offshore banking, plays a significant role in the islands' economy.

Preserving the natural environment and cultural heritage is a priority in St. Kitts and Nevis. Efforts are made to protect the islands' fragile ecosystems, including coral reefs and rainforests, through the establishment of national parks and marine reserves. The people of St. Kitts and Nevis take pride in their rich history and work towards ensuring the sustainable development and preservation of their treasured islands.

St. Kitts and Nevis, with their distinction as the first British colony in the Caribbean, offer a captivating blend of history, natural beauty, and cultural richness. The islands' unique heritage and warm island charm create an unforgettable experience for visitors, inviting them to explore the past, immerse themselves in the present, and savor the allure of this Caribbean gem.

St. Lucia: Pitons, Rainforests, and Creole Culture

St. Lucia, a captivating island in the eastern Caribbean, is known for its iconic Pitons, lush rainforests, and vibrant Creole culture. This chapter unveils the natural wonders, cultural heritage, and unique charm that define St. Lucia, painting a vivid picture of this Caribbean gem.

The Pitons, two towering volcanic peaks, are the most recognizable symbols of St. Lucia. Gros Piton and Petit Piton rise dramatically from the sea, creating a stunning backdrop against the island's lush landscapes. These UNESCO World Heritage-listed landmarks are a sight to behold and attract visitors from around the world. Hiking to the summit of the Pitons offers breathtaking panoramic views of the surrounding turquoise waters and verdant landscapes.

St. Lucia's natural beauty extends far beyond the Pitons. The island boasts pristine white-sand beaches, hidden coves, and crystal-clear waters that entice beach lovers and water enthusiasts alike. Anse Chastanet, Reduit Beach, and Marigot Bay are just a few examples of the stunning coastal destinations that showcase the island's paradise-like scenery.

The rainforests of St. Lucia are a treasure trove of biodiversity. The lush foliage, cascading waterfalls, and meandering rivers create a haven for flora and fauna. The Edmund Rainforest Reserve offers opportunities for hiking and exploring the island's rich ecological wonders. The Diamond Falls Botanical Gardens, with its vibrant array of tropical flowers and therapeutic mineral baths, provide a serene escape into nature's embrace.

Creole culture is deeply ingrained in the fabric of St. Lucian society. The island's population is a vibrant mix of African, European, and indigenous Carib heritage, creating a fusion of traditions, languages, and culinary delights. The Creole language, a unique blend of French and African languages, is widely spoken and adds a distinctive touch to the cultural landscape.

Music and dance are integral parts of St. Lucian culture. The island's rhythms, such as soca, calypso, and reggae, resonate through lively festivals and celebratory events. The annual St. Lucia Jazz Festival attracts renowned local and international musicians, infusing the island with melodious vibes and showcasing the talent of St. Lucian artists.

Culinary delights await food enthusiasts in St. Lucia. Creole cuisine tantalizes the taste buds with its vibrant flavors and fresh ingredients. Local dishes like callaloo soup, green fig and saltfish, and bouyon (a hearty meat and vegetable stew) showcase the island's unique blend of African, French, and indigenous influences. The aroma of spices, such as nutmeg, cinnamon, and allspice, fills the air, adding depth and richness to St. Lucian culinary traditions.

St. Lucia's commitment to preserving its natural heritage is evident in its efforts to protect its marine ecosystems and rainforests. The Soufrière Marine Management Area safeguards the island's coral reefs, ensuring their sustainability for future generations. The Forestry Department works tirelessly to preserve the island's rainforests, educating visitors about their importance and implementing sustainable practices.

The warmth and hospitality of the St. Lucian people create a welcoming atmosphere for visitors. The island's tourism industry plays a vital role in its economy, offering a range of accommodations, from luxury resorts to eco-friendly boutique hotels. Soufrière, with its charming colonial architecture, and Rodney Bay, known for its vibrant nightlife and entertainment options, are popular destinations for travelers seeking relaxation, adventure, or a blend of both.

St. Lucia's enchanting beauty, diverse ecosystems, and rich cultural heritage combine to create an immersive experience for those who venture to its shores. Whether it's hiking through rainforests, snorkeling among coral reefs, or indulging in the flavors of Creole cuisine, St. Lucia entices with its natural wonders and vibrant spirit, leaving an indelible impression on all who explore its diverse offerings.

Antigua and Barbuda: Sailing Capital of the Caribbean

Antigua and Barbuda, a stunning twin-island nation in the Caribbean, holds the title of the Sailing Capital of the Caribbean. This chapter explores the allure of Antigua and Barbuda, from its rich maritime heritage to its breathtaking landscapes and vibrant sailing culture, painting a vivid picture of this nautical paradise.

The islands of Antigua and Barbuda have a long-standing association with sailing. The sheltered harbors, steady trade winds, and crystal-clear waters make these islands a sailor's dream. It is no wonder that Antigua and Barbuda have become a mecca for sailing enthusiasts from around the world.

Antigua, the larger of the two islands, boasts an impressive array of harbors, marinas, and anchorages that cater to all types of sailing vessels. Nelson's Dockyard, a UNESCO World Heritage site, located in English Harbour, stands as a testament to the island's maritime heritage. This historic naval base, once frequented by Admiral Horatio Nelson, has been beautifully restored and now serves as a hub for yachting activities.

The annual Antigua Sailing Week, held every April, is one of the most renowned sailing events in the Caribbean. This week-long regatta attracts sailors, yacht owners, and spectators from all corners of the globe. The races showcase a range of sailing classes, from sleek racing yachts to traditional island sloops, creating a thrilling spectacle on the azure waters surrounding the islands.

Beyond the sailing events, Antigua's coast is adorned with stunning beaches that offer picturesque anchorages and postcard-perfect views. From the popular Dickenson Bay and Jolly Harbour to the secluded shores of Half Moon Bay and Rendezvous Bay, there is no shortage of idyllic spots to drop anchor, swim, or simply relax under the warm Caribbean sun.

Barbuda, the smaller sister island, presents a more serene and untouched sailing experience. With its unspoiled beaches, such as Pink Beach and Coco Point, and the expansive Frigate Bird Sanctuary, Barbuda offers a tranquil escape for sailors seeking solitude and natural beauty.

The islands' sailing culture is deeply embedded in the daily life of Antiguans and Barbudans. Traditional boat-building techniques, passed down through generations, continue to thrive. Local wooden sailboats, known as "Carriacou Sloops" or "Antigua Sloops," reflect the islands' seafaring heritage and are often seen gracefully gliding across the waters during races and festivals.

The passion for sailing extends to the hospitality industry, with numerous resorts, hotels, and yacht clubs catering to sailors and providing facilities for both land-based and sea-based activities. Luxury marinas, such as Falmouth Harbour Marina and Antigua Yacht Club Marina, offer world-class amenities and services to accommodate visiting yachts.

Antigua and Barbuda's commitment to marine conservation is evident in the establishment of marine parks and protected areas. The North Sound Marine Park, located off the northeastern coast of Antigua, is a haven for marine life and offers excellent snorkeling and diving opportunities. The pristine coral reefs, vibrant fish species, and even the occasional sighting of sea turtles contribute to the allure of these protected waters.

The islands' beauty and sailing reputation have not gone unnoticed in the film industry. Numerous movies, including the famous "Pirates of the Caribbean" series, have chosen Antigua and Barbuda as filming locations, captivated by the cinematic backdrops provided by the islands' natural splendor.

Sailing in Antigua and Barbuda is not limited to seasoned sailors. The islands offer a range of sailing excursions, day trips, and charters, allowing visitors of all skill levels to experience the joy of being on the water. Whether it's a leisurely sunset cruise, a thrilling catamaran adventure, or a hands-on sailing lesson, there is something for everyone to enjoy.

The charm of Antigua and Barbuda extends beyond the sailing scene. The islands boast a vibrant culture, warm hospitality, and a rich historical heritage. The capital city of St. John's on Antigua offers a blend of traditional Caribbean charm and modern amenities, with bustling markets, colonial architecture, and a lively atmosphere. The quaint village of Codrington on Barbuda provides a glimpse into the island's quieter pace of life, with its charming streets and friendly locals.

The cuisine of Antigua and Barbuda reflects the islands' cultural diversity and abundance of fresh seafood. Local specialties, such as pepperpot, saltfish and fungi, and conch fritters, showcase the flavors of the Caribbean with a unique Antiguan twist. Restaurants and beachside shacks offer a delectable array of culinary delights, ranging from traditional Creole dishes to international fusion cuisine.

Antigua and Barbuda's enchanting combination of natural beauty, vibrant sailing culture, and warm hospitality create an irresistible allure for sailors and visitors alike. Whether one chooses to navigate the azure waters, lounge on the picturesque beaches, or immerse themselves in the islands' rich cultural heritage, Antigua and Barbuda beckon with their maritime charm and nautical wonders.

St. Vincent and the Grenadines: The Land of the Pirates

St. Vincent and the Grenadines, a captivating archipelago in the Caribbean, holds a fascinating history intertwined with tales of pirates and buccaneers. This chapter delves into the allure of St. Vincent and the Grenadines, exploring its pirate-infused past, stunning landscapes, and vibrant cultural heritage, painting a vivid picture of this captivating land.

The islands of St. Vincent and the Grenadines were once a haven for pirates who roamed the Caribbean seas. The rugged terrain, hidden coves, and strategic location made them an ideal base for pirates seeking refuge and a place to hide their treasures. The surrounding waters, dotted with numerous islets and secluded anchorages, provided ample opportunities for pirates to ambush unsuspecting ships.

One notable pirate associated with St. Vincent and the Grenadines is the infamous Blackbeard, also known as Edward Teach. Legend has it that Blackbeard used the islands as a base for his piratical activities, terrorizing merchant vessels in the surrounding waters. His menacing appearance, with a long black beard and smoking fuses tucked into his hat, struck fear into the hearts of his victims.

The coastal areas of St. Vincent and the Grenadines still bear the remnants of their piratical past. Hidden caves, such as Blackbeard's Cave on St. Vincent, are believed to have served as pirate hideouts. The dark, mysterious chambers of these caves evoke a sense of adventure and intrigue, inviting visitors to imagine the stories that unfolded within their walls.

Beyond its pirate legacy, St. Vincent and the Grenadines offer a wealth of natural beauty. St. Vincent, the largest island, is characterized by lush rainforests, cascading waterfalls, and volcanic landscapes. The iconic Soufrière volcano, known as La Soufrière, stands as a prominent landmark, shrouded in myth and mystery.

The Grenadines, a collection of picturesque islands and cays, present a paradise-like setting. Bequia, Mustique, and Union Island are just a few examples of the stunning destinations that showcase the Grenadines' pristine beaches, crystal-clear waters, and unspoiled beauty. The Tobago Cays Marine Park, a protected area, offers a unique opportunity to snorkel among vibrant coral reefs and swim alongside sea turtles.

Cultural heritage is deeply rooted in the fabric of St. Vincent and the Grenadines. The indigenous Garifuna people, also known as the Garifuna, have a rich history and cultural traditions that blend African, European, and indigenous influences. Their vibrant music, dance, and storytelling reflect the resilience and spirit of the Garifuna people.

Music plays a significant role in St. Vincent and the Grenadines' cultural landscape. Calypso, soca, and reggae rhythms permeate the air during the annual Vincy Mas Carnival, a vibrant celebration of music, dance, and cultural pride. Steel pan music, with its melodious tones, adds a distinct Caribbean flavor to the island's musical tapestry.

The cuisine of St. Vincent and the Grenadines is a delicious reflection of the islands' cultural diversity. Local dishes like roasted breadfruit, callaloo soup, and fried jackfish showcase the flavors of the Caribbean with a unique Vincy twist. The bustling Kingstown Market is a treasure trove of fresh fruits, vegetables, spices, and local crafts, providing a sensory feast for visitors.

St. Vincent and the Grenadines have made efforts to preserve their natural and cultural heritage. The Vermont Nature Trail and the Montreal Gardens on St. Vincent offer opportunities for visitors to explore the islands' rich biodiversity and tropical flora. The Breadfruit Institute, located on St. Vincent, works towards the conservation and promotion of the breadfruit tree, a significant cultural and culinary symbol.

The warm hospitality of the Vincentian people adds a special touch to the island experience. Whether it's visiting a local rum shop, engaging in lively conversations, or participating in traditional festivals, visitors are welcomed with open arms and embraced by the vibrant spirit of the Vincentian community.

St. Vincent and the Grenadines' pirate legacy, combined with its breathtaking landscapes and vibrant cultural heritage, create an irresistible allure for adventurers and history enthusiasts. Whether one seeks to uncover hidden caves, explore volcanic landscapes, or simply soak up the laid-back Caribbean vibes, St. Vincent and the Grenadines invite all to embark on a journey through their captivating and piratical past.

The Cayman Islands: Tax Havens and Marine Life

The Cayman Islands, a trio of idyllic islands in the Caribbean Sea, are known for their status as international financial centers and their rich marine life. This chapter explores the unique blend of tax havens and natural wonders that define the Cayman Islands, providing an insight into their economic significance and the diverse marine ecosystems that surround them.

The Cayman Islands have gained global recognition as a leading offshore financial center. Their favorable tax policies, stable economy, and well-regulated financial sector have attracted businesses and individuals from around the world. The islands' status as tax havens has contributed to their economic prosperity, making them an attractive destination for international investment and financial services.

Grand Cayman, the largest of the three islands, is the main hub for offshore financial activities. The island boasts numerous international banks, accounting firms, and legal services that cater to the needs of global clients. The Cayman Islands' business-friendly environment, political stability, and strong legal framework have positioned them as a trusted jurisdiction for financial transactions and asset management.

It is important to note that while the Cayman Islands are renowned for their financial sector, they are also committed to international standards of transparency and regulation. The islands have implemented measures to combat money laundering, tax evasion, and other illicit activities. The Cayman Islands Monetary Authority oversees the financial industry, ensuring compliance with international standards and maintaining the integrity of the jurisdiction.

Beyond their financial reputation, the Cayman Islands are home to some of the most spectacular marine environments in the Caribbean. The crystal-clear waters, vibrant coral reefs, and diverse marine life attract snorkelers, divers, and nature enthusiasts from all corners of the globe. The islands boast an abundance of marine protected areas, including the famous Stingray City, where visitors can interact with gentle stingrays in their natural habitat.

The underwater world of the Cayman Islands is teeming with life. Colorful coral formations, including delicate fan corals and impressive brain corals, create a vibrant backdrop for a vast array of marine species. Snorkelers and divers can encounter tropical fish of all sizes, from tiny gobies and angelfish to majestic eagle rays and reef sharks. The islands are also known for their impressive wall dives, where divers can explore dramatic drop-offs into the depths of the Caribbean Sea.

One of the highlights of the Cayman Islands' marine life is the annual migration of the magnificent whale sharks. These gentle giants, the largest fish in the ocean, visit the waters of the Cayman Islands between May and September, offering a rare opportunity for divers to swim alongside these majestic creatures. The Cayman Islands have implemented regulations to protect the whale sharks and ensure responsible interactions with them.

The commitment to marine conservation is evident in the Cayman Islands' efforts to preserve their delicate ecosystems. The islands have established marine parks and protected areas, such as the Bloody Bay Marine Park and the Queen Elizabeth II Botanic Park, to safeguard their natural heritage. These conservation initiatives aim to maintain the health of the coral reefs, protect endangered species, and promote sustainable tourism practices.

While the financial sector and marine life are key aspects of the Cayman Islands, the islands also offer a range of other attractions. Seven Mile Beach on Grand Cayman is a world-renowned stretch of pristine white sand, lined with luxury resorts, restaurants, and water sports facilities. Cayman Brac and Little Cayman, the two sister islands, provide a more tranquil and laid-back experience, with opportunities for nature exploration, birdwatching, and relaxing on secluded beaches.

The cultural heritage of the Cayman Islands is a reflection of its diverse population, which includes Caymanians, expatriates, and immigrants from various backgrounds. The islands' heritage is celebrated through festivals, such as Pirates Week, which pays homage to the islands' pirate history, and Batabano, a colorful carnival showcasing music, dance, and local traditions.

Cuisine in the Cayman Islands is a fusion of international flavors and local ingredients. The islands boast a vibrant culinary scene, with restaurants offering a variety of cuisines, from fresh seafood to Caribbean-inspired dishes. The famous Caymanian dish, "turtle stew," once a traditional staple, is now a protected species, and its consumption is strictly regulated.

The Cayman Islands' unique combination of tax havens and marine life creates a distinct identity that sets them apart from other Caribbean destinations. The islands' economic prosperity and natural beauty have positioned them as a sought-after destination for both business and leisure travelers. Whether it's conducting financial transactions or exploring the vibrant underwater world, the Cayman Islands offer a unique experience that combines economic opportunities with the splendors of nature's bounty.

The British Virgin Islands: Sailors' Paradise

The British Virgin Islands, a pristine archipelago in the Caribbean Sea, have earned a well-deserved reputation as a sailors' paradise. This chapter unravels the allure of the British Virgin Islands, exploring their breathtaking beauty, world-class sailing conditions, and the unique experiences they offer to sailing enthusiasts from around the globe.

The British Virgin Islands (BVIs) comprise more than 60 islands and cays, each with its own distinctive charm. The main islands, including Tortola, Virgin Gorda, Anegada, and Jost Van Dyke, are renowned for their stunning landscapes, azure waters, and serene anchorages. The BVIs' strategic location, nestled among the northeastern Caribbean islands, ensures consistent trade winds and calm seas, creating ideal conditions for sailing throughout the year.

Sailing is deeply embedded in the culture and lifestyle of the British Virgin Islands. The islands' rich maritime heritage, dating back to the days of pirate lore and British colonization, has shaped their identity as a nautical destination. The BVIs' sheltered bays, hidden coves, and pristine beaches provide endless opportunities for exploration, relaxation, and adventure on the water.

The BVIs offer a range of sailing experiences suitable for all levels of expertise. Bareboat charters, where individuals or groups can rent a sailboat or catamaran and captain it themselves, are a popular option for experienced sailors. Crewed charters, on the other hand, provide a luxurious and hassle-free sailing experience, with professional crew members attending to guests' every need.

The famous trade winds that sweep across the Caribbean ensure exhilarating sailing adventures in the BVIs. The consistent easterly winds, blowing between 10 to 20 knots, propel sailboats gracefully through the turquoise waters. The Sir Francis Drake Channel, a picturesque waterway that separates the BVIs' main islands, presents an ideal setting for exhilarating races, leisurely cruises, or peaceful sunset sails.

Navigating through the BVIs reveals a myriad of captivating destinations. The Baths, located on the island of Virgin Gorda, is an iconic natural wonder, featuring giant granite boulders forming scenic grottoes and pools. This unique geological formation provides an extraordinary backdrop for snorkeling, swimming, and exploring hidden passages.

Jost Van Dyke, a small island with a laid-back vibe, is famous for its lively beach bars and the world-renowned Soggy Dollar Bar. The pristine White Bay, lined with powdery white sand and swaying palm trees, entices visitors to relax, swim, and indulge in refreshing cocktails.

Norman Island, often believed to be the inspiration for Robert Louis Stevenson's novel "Treasure Island," is a captivating destination for snorkelers and divers. The island is surrounded by a coral reef, which is home to an array of marine life and the legendary underwater caves known as "The Caves."

Anegada, a coral atoll situated northeast of the main BVIs, offers a unique sailing experience with its low-lying, sandy terrain. Known for its pristine beaches and abundant wildlife, Anegada attracts nature enthusiasts, beachcombers, and those seeking a tranquil escape.

The BVIs' commitment to marine conservation is evident through the establishment of protected areas and the promotion of sustainable practices. The BVI National Parks Trust oversees several marine parks, including the famous Wreck of the RMS Rhone, a popular dive site and a historical treasure. These protected areas preserve the islands' delicate marine ecosystems, ensuring their longevity for future generations.

The BVIs' onshore offerings complement the sailing experience, providing opportunities to explore the islands' rich history, vibrant culture, and local cuisine. Road Town, the capital of the BVIs on Tortola, showcases colonial architecture, quaint shops, and lively markets, where visitors can immerse themselves in the local culture and purchase unique crafts and souvenirs.

Cultural events, such as the BVI Spring Regatta and Music Festival, unite sailing enthusiasts and music lovers from around the world. This annual event combines thrilling sailing races with live music performances, creating a lively atmosphere of celebration and camaraderie.

The culinary scene in the BVIs reflects the islands' diverse influences, blending Caribbean flavors with international cuisine. Fresh seafood, including lobster, conch, and fish, takes center stage in many traditional dishes. Local beachside restaurants, known as "beach shacks," serve up delectable meals, offering a fusion of flavors that cater to every palate.

The natural beauty, favorable sailing conditions, and warm hospitality of the British Virgin Islands make it a destination that captures the hearts of sailors and adventurers alike. The harmonious balance between serenity and excitement, both on the water and on land, creates a truly unparalleled experience for those seeking the ultimate sailing getaway.

The U.S. Virgin Islands: American Caribbean Delights

The U.S. Virgin Islands, a captivating group of islands in the Caribbean Sea, offer a unique blend of American influence and Caribbean charm. This chapter explores the allure of the U.S. Virgin Islands, from their breathtaking landscapes and vibrant culture to their status as an unincorporated territory of the United States.

The U.S. Virgin Islands consist of three main islands: St. Thomas, St. John, and St. Croix. Each island has its own distinct character, yet all share the warm hospitality and natural beauty that define the U.S. Virgin Islands as a whole.

St. Thomas, the most cosmopolitan of the islands, is known for its bustling capital, Charlotte Amalie. This vibrant city is a hub of activity, with its duty-free shopping, historic sites, and lively waterfront. Visitors can explore the iconic Blackbeard's Castle, visit the renowned Coral World Ocean Park, or simply stroll along the charming streets lined with colorful buildings and quaint shops.

St. John, known as the "Gem of the Caribbean," captivates visitors with its pristine beauty and untouched landscapes. The majority of the island is protected as part of the Virgin Islands National Park, ensuring the preservation of its remarkable natural treasures. Trunk Bay, with its picture-perfect beach and underwater snorkeling trail, is often ranked among the world's most beautiful beaches.

St. Croix, the largest of the U.S. Virgin Islands, boasts a rich history and a vibrant culture. The town of Christiansted, with its charming Danish colonial architecture, showcases the island's historical heritage. Visitors can explore the historic sites, such as Fort Christiansvaern and the Christiansted National Historic Site, which offer insights into the island's colonial past.

The U.S. Virgin Islands offer a wide range of outdoor activities and water sports. Sailing, snorkeling, diving, and fishing are popular pursuits, thanks to the crystal-clear waters and abundant marine life. The underwater world surrounding the islands is a paradise for divers, with vibrant coral reefs, colorful tropical fish, and the occasional sighting of sea turtles and rays.

Cultural diversity is a hallmark of the U.S. Virgin Islands. The islands are home to a blend of African, European, and American influences, which is reflected in their music, art, and cuisine. The annual Carnival celebrations, held in the spring, showcase the vibrant spirit of the islands, with colorful parades, music, dance, and traditional costumes.

The U.S. Virgin Islands are an unincorporated territory of the United States, which grants them a unique status. While the islands enjoy many of the benefits and protections of being part of the United States, they also maintain their own distinct identity and local government. The U.S. dollar is the official currency, and English is the primary language spoken throughout the islands.

Tourism plays a vital role in the economy of the U.S. Virgin Islands. The islands welcome millions of visitors each year, drawn by the stunning natural beauty, warm climate, and the convenience of being part of the United States. The tourism industry provides employment opportunities and contributes significantly to the islands' infrastructure and development.

The U.S. Virgin Islands' cuisine is a delightful fusion of Caribbean flavors and American influences. Local dishes, such as conch fritters, johnnycakes, and goat water stew, highlight the culinary heritage of the islands. Visitors can indulge in a wide array of dining options, from beachside shacks serving up fresh seafood to fine dining establishments offering international cuisine.

The U.S. Virgin Islands' status as an American territory ensures access to modern amenities and infrastructure, including healthcare facilities, reliable transportation, and telecommunications. The islands have a well-established education system and provide a high standard of living for residents and visitors alike.

The U.S. Virgin Islands, with their blend of American conveniences and Caribbean delights, offer a captivating experience for travelers seeking a tropical getaway with a touch of familiarity. From the vibrant streets of St. Thomas to the unspoiled beauty of St. John and the historical charm of St. Croix, the U.S. Virgin Islands enchant visitors with their unique blend of cultures, stunning landscapes, and warm hospitality.

Belize: Barrier Reefs and Ancient Maya Ruins

Belize, a mesmerizing country located on the eastern coast of Central America, is renowned for its magnificent barrier reefs and ancient Maya ruins. This chapter delves into the captivating allure of Belize, exploring its diverse ecosystems, rich cultural heritage, and the fascinating blend of natural wonders and archaeological treasures that make it a truly unique destination.

At the heart of Belize's natural wonders lies the Belize Barrier Reef, a UNESCO World Heritage Site and the largest barrier reef system in the Northern Hemisphere. Stretching over 190 miles (300 kilometers) along the country's coastline, the reef is a haven for marine life and a paradise for divers and snorkelers. Its crystal-clear waters teem with vibrant coral formations, mesmerizing tropical fish, and intriguing marine creatures like sea turtles, rays, and nurse sharks.

The reef's biodiversity is a testament to Belize's commitment to conservation. Protected areas, such as the Hol Chan Marine Reserve and the Blue Hole Natural Monument, safeguard the fragile ecosystems and offer visitors the opportunity to explore underwater caves, swim with whale sharks (seasonally), and witness the wonders of the marine world. Beyond its turquoise waters, Belize boasts a remarkable wealth of terrestrial beauty. The country is home to pristine rainforests, lush jungles, and majestic rivers. The Cockscomb Basin Wildlife Sanctuary, also known as the Jaguar Preserve, provides a sanctuary for the elusive jaguars, along with a plethora of other wildlife species. Nature enthusiasts can embark on exhilarating hikes, birdwatching adventures, and river explorations, immersing themselves in the country's abundant flora and fauna. Belize's rich cultural heritage is deeply intertwined with the remnants of the ancient Maya civilization. The country boasts an impressive collection of Maya ruins, providing a glimpse into the remarkable achievements of this advanced civilization. Sites such as Caracol, Xunantunich, and Lamanai showcase majestic pyramids, intricately carved stelae, and sprawling plazas, all bearing witness to the grandeur and architectural prowess of the Maya people.

The ruins of Altun Ha, with its famous Jade Head, and the mystical caves of Actun Tunichil Muknal (ATM Cave) add further intrigue to Belize's archaeological landscape. These sites provide an opportunity to immerse oneself in the mysteries of the Maya world, discovering ancient artifacts, sacred chambers, and ceremonial remains that have withstood the test of time.

The Maya civilization not only left behind awe-inspiring architectural wonders but also a rich cultural legacy. Indigenous Maya communities, such as the Kekchi and Mopan, continue to preserve their traditions, language, and vibrant customs. Visitors can engage in immersive cultural experiences, from participating in traditional ceremonies to learning about Maya herbal medicine and craftmaking.

Belize's cultural diversity extends beyond its Maya heritage. The country is home to a mix of ethnicities, including Creole, Garifuna, Mestizo, and Mennonite communities. Each group contributes to Belize's cultural tapestry through its unique traditions, music, dance, and cuisine.

The local cuisine of Belize reflects the country's cultural fusion. Influences from Maya, Creole, Garifuna, and Mestizo traditions blend to create a tantalizing array of flavors. From hearty stews and fresh seafood to delicious tamales and flavorful rice and beans, Belizean cuisine tantalizes the taste buds with its diverse culinary offerings.

Belize's commitment to sustainable tourism and conservation is evident in its extensive protected areas and eco-friendly initiatives. The country has designated more than 40% of its land as protected areas, including national parks, wildlife sanctuaries, and marine reserves. These efforts ensure the preservation of Belize's natural heritage for future generations to cherish.

The warmth and hospitality of the Belizean people add an extra dimension to the country's charm. Known for their friendly nature and welcoming spirit, Belizeans embrace visitors with open arms, sharing their cultural traditions and stories, and inviting them to experience the beauty and wonder of their homeland.

Belize, with its combination of barrier reefs, ancient Maya ruins, lush rainforests, and diverse cultures, offers a captivating journey of exploration and discovery. Whether it's diving into the vibrant underwater world, trekking through the jungles in search of ancient wonders, or immersing oneself in the cultural tapestry of the country, Belize promises an unforgettable adventure that seamlessly blends natural beauty, historical significance, and warm hospitality.

Aruba: One Happy Island in the Caribbean

Aruba, a captivating island nestled in the southern Caribbean Sea, is often referred to as "One Happy Island." This chapter explores the unique appeal of Aruba, delving into its stunning landscapes, vibrant culture, and the warm hospitality that welcomes visitors from around the world.

Aruba's picturesque beauty is evident in its pristine beaches, turquoise waters, and rugged desert-like terrain. Palm-lined white sand beaches, such as Eagle Beach and Palm Beach, invite visitors to relax under the shade of swaying trees and soak up the Caribbean sun. The island's constant trade winds provide a refreshing breeze and make it a paradise for windsurfing and kitesurfing enthusiasts.

The island's natural wonders extend beyond its shores. Arikok National Park, covering approximately 18% of Aruba's land area, showcases its unique desert-like landscapes, towering cacti, dramatic rock formations, and hidden caves. Visitors can explore the park's hiking trails, encounter native wildlife, and discover the rich cultural history of the island.

Aruba's cultural heritage is a fusion of influences from its indigenous roots, Spanish and Dutch colonial history, and the diverse backgrounds of its people. The local language, Papiamento, reflects this blend of cultures and serves as a symbol of national identity. English and Dutch are also widely spoken on the island.

The capital city of Oranjestad offers a glimpse into Aruba's colonial past through its charming architecture, colorful buildings, and historical sites. Fort Zoutman, the oldest structure on the island, is now home to the Aruba Historical Museum, where visitors can learn about the island's history, traditions, and customs.

Aruba's commitment to preserving its natural environment is evident in its sustainable practices and conservation efforts. The island has implemented initiatives to protect its marine life and coral reefs, including designated marine parks and artificial reef systems. The Aruba Reef Care Project engages the community in beach clean-ups and reef restoration activities, ensuring the long-term health of Aruba's coastal ecosystems.

The warmth and friendliness of the Aruban people contribute to the island's reputation as "One Happy Island." The locals, known as "Arubans," embrace visitors with genuine hospitality and a welcoming spirit. The island's cultural festivals, such as Carnival and Dera Gai (Harvest Festival), showcase the vibrant music, dance, and traditions of the Aruban people.

Aruba's culinary scene tantalizes the taste buds with its diverse flavors and influences. The island's cuisine combines traditional Aruban dishes with international influences, creating a unique culinary experience. Visitors can savor local specialties such as keshi yena (stuffed cheese), fresh seafood delicacies, and a variety of Caribbean-inspired dishes.

The tourism industry plays a vital role in Aruba's economy, providing employment opportunities and driving the island's development. Aruba's infrastructure, including its modern resorts, hotels, and amenities, cater to the needs of travelers seeking relaxation, adventure, and exploration. The island's accessibility, with direct flights from various international destinations, makes it a popular vacation spot for visitors from around the world.

Aruba's commitment to sustainability and responsible tourism is demonstrated through its Green Globe certification, renewable energy initiatives, and eco-friendly practices. The island strives to minimize its environmental impact and protect its natural resources for future generations to enjoy.

Aruba's tagline, "One Happy Island," encapsulates the island's unwavering dedication to ensuring a memorable and joyful experience for its visitors. From its stunning beaches and captivating landscapes to its vibrant culture and warm hospitality, Aruba invites travelers to embrace the spirit of happiness and create lasting memories on this idyllic Caribbean island.

The Turks and Caicos Islands: Hidden Gems of the Caribbean

The Turks and Caicos Islands, a captivating archipelago located in the Lucayan Archipelago of the Atlantic Ocean, are often regarded as the hidden gems of the Caribbean. This chapter explores the allure of the Turks and Caicos Islands, delving into their pristine beaches, crystal-clear waters, and the tranquil atmosphere that attracts discerning travelers seeking an idyllic escape.

Comprising 40 islands and cays, the Turks and Caicos Islands offer a diverse range of natural wonders and breathtaking landscapes. Providenciales, commonly known as Provo, is the most developed and popular island, renowned for its stunning Grace Bay Beach. With its powdery white sand and vibrant turquoise waters, Grace Bay Beach consistently ranks among the world's best beaches.

Beyond Grace Bay, the Turks and Caicos Islands offer a treasure trove of secluded beaches and hidden coves waiting to be discovered. From the untouched beauty of Long Bay Beach to the tranquility of Taylor Bay, these pristine shores provide an intimate and peaceful retreat for visitors seeking solace and relaxation.

The islands' world-class coral reefs and vibrant marine life make them a haven for snorkeling and diving enthusiasts. The Turks and Caicos Barrier Reef, the third-largest coral reef system in the world, stretches along the eastern edge of the islands. Exploring its underwater wonders reveals a kaleidoscope of colorful coral formations, tropical fish, and the occasional sighting of graceful sea turtles and majestic manta rays.

The Turks and Caicos Islands' commitment to environmental preservation is evident through their marine parks and protected areas. The Princess Alexandra National Park, encompassing Grace Bay and its surrounding waters, ensures the conservation of the islands' coastal ecosystems. It serves as a sanctuary for endangered species such as the hawksbill turtle and serves as a nesting ground for seabirds.

The islands' natural beauty extends beyond their shores. The interior landscapes of islands like Middle Caicos and North Caicos feature picturesque rolling hills, dense mangrove wetlands, and hidden limestone caves waiting to be explored. The famous Conch Bar Caves, a vast underground system, offer a unique adventure for spelunkers and nature enthusiasts.

The Turks and Caicos Islands' rich history is intertwined with the Lucayan people, the islands' original inhabitants. The Lucayans, an indigenous Arawak-speaking people, settled in the islands around 700 AD. Christopher Columbus is believed to have encountered the Lucayans during his voyages in the late 15th century. Today, remnants of the Lucayan culture can be seen in archaeological sites such as Cheshire Hall on Providenciales.

The islands' colonial history, predominantly influenced by the British, shaped their current political structure as a British Overseas Territory. English is the official language, and the islands' legal system, education, and governance follow British traditions. The Turks and

Caicos Islands maintain a distinct sense of British heritage while embracing their Caribbean identity.

The cuisine of the Turks and Caicos Islands reflects their cultural influences, combining fresh seafood, local produce, and international flavors. From the succulent flavors of conch dishes to the aromatic spices used in Caribbean-inspired cuisine, the islands' culinary offerings provide a delightful exploration of taste and texture.

The tourism industry plays a significant role in the Turks and Caicos Islands' economy, providing employment opportunities and contributing to the islands' development. Luxury resorts, boutique hotels, and private villas cater to the discerning tastes of travelers seeking a serene and exclusive getaway. The islands' pristine natural environment, coupled with the warm hospitality of the local population, creates an atmosphere of tranquility and indulgence.

While the Turks and Caicos Islands may be considered hidden gems, they continue to garner international acclaim for their natural beauty, world-class beaches, and commitment to environmental conservation. The islands' serene atmosphere, coupled with their unspoiled landscapes, make them an ideal destination for those seeking a peaceful retreat amidst the splendor of the Caribbean.

Whether it's exploring the vibrant underwater world, basking in the sun on secluded beaches, or simply immersing oneself in the laid-back island lifestyle, the Turks and Caicos Islands offer an enchanting escape where visitors can discover their own slice of paradise in the Caribbean.

Diving into the Depths: Exploring Caribbean Marine Life

The Caribbean Sea is renowned for its rich biodiversity and vibrant underwater ecosystems. This chapter delves into the captivating world of Caribbean marine life, exploring the diverse array of species that inhabit its waters, the importance of coral reefs, and the thrill of exploring the depths through diving and snorkeling.

The Caribbean is home to an astounding variety of marine life, ranging from colorful tropical fish and majestic sea turtles to elusive sharks and graceful rays. The warm, nutrient-rich waters of the region provide an ideal habitat for an abundance of species, making it a paradise for divers and snorkelers seeking an up-close encounter with nature.

Coral reefs are the lifeblood of the Caribbean's marine ecosystems. These intricate, living structures provide shelter, food, and breeding grounds for a multitude of species. The vibrant colors and delicate formations of coral reefs create a mesmerizing underwater landscape that attracts both marine life and those who seek to explore their beauty.

The Caribbean boasts some of the world's most iconic coral reefs, including the Great Barrier Reef in Belize, the Gardens of the Queen in Cuba, and the Tobago Cays Marine Park in St. Vincent and the Grenadines. These protected areas offer a glimpse into the stunning diversity of coral species, as well as the opportunity to encounter a kaleidoscope of marine creatures.

One of the most beloved inhabitants of the Caribbean Sea is the sea turtle. Several species of sea turtles, including the green turtle, hawksbill turtle, and loggerhead turtle, call the Caribbean home. These graceful creatures are not only a delight to observe but also play a crucial role in maintaining the health of the coral reefs, as they help control the growth of algae.

Sharks, often portrayed as fearsome predators, are an essential part of the Caribbean's marine ecosystem. While encounters with sharks may evoke a mix of awe and caution, it's important to note that the majority of shark species found in the Caribbean are harmless to humans. The Caribbean is home to species such as nurse sharks, reef sharks, and even the majestic whale shark, the largest fish in the sea.

The Caribbean's vibrant fish population is a sight to behold. Schools of colorful reef fish, such as parrotfish, angelfish, and butterflyfish, adorn the coral reefs, creating a spectacle of movement and color. Other notable inhabitants include the charismatic clownfish, known for its symbiotic relationship with anemones, and the elusive and clever octopus, which showcases incredible camouflage skills.

Beyond the coral reefs, the Caribbean offers a diverse array of underwater landscapes to explore. Seagrass beds provide essential nurseries for many marine species, including juvenile fish and sea turtles. Mangrove forests, with their intertwining roots and dense vegetation, serve as breeding grounds and shelter for various marine creatures, acting as vital coastal ecosystems.

Diving and snorkeling are popular activities in the Caribbean, attracting enthusiasts from around the world. The region's warm waters, excellent visibility, and a wide range of dive sites cater to divers of all skill levels. From vibrant shallow reefs to thrilling deep-sea walls and wreck dives, the Caribbean offers a myriad of underwater adventures to suit every diver's preference.

The Caribbean is also a pioneer in marine conservation efforts. Many countries in the region have established marine parks and protected areas to safeguard their precious marine ecosystems. These initiatives aim to preserve coral reefs, regulate fishing practices, and promote sustainable tourism, ensuring that future generations can continue to appreciate the beauty and abundance of Caribbean marine life.

In recent years, awareness of the importance of marine conservation has increased, and efforts to combat plastic pollution and promote responsible tourism have gained momentum. The Caribbean community, along with local and international organizations, is working tirelessly to protect the region's marine resources and raise awareness about the fragile balance of its underwater ecosystems.

Diving into the depths of the Caribbean reveals a world teeming with life and wonder. It allows us to appreciate the interconnectedness of marine species, the importance of preserving coral reefs, and the delicate balance of nature. Exploring the underwater realm of the Caribbean is an invitation to witness the marvels of the sea and to become stewards of its preservation.

Wildlife Wonders: Flora and Fauna of the Caribbean

The Caribbean region is not only renowned for its stunning beaches and vibrant culture but also for its rich and diverse array of flora and fauna. This chapter explores the fascinating world of Caribbean wildlife, from lush rainforests and mangrove swamps to the unique animal species that call this region home.

The Caribbean's natural landscapes are characterized by a variety of ecosystems, each supporting its own unique flora and fauna. The region's tropical climate, abundant rainfall, and fertile soil create ideal conditions for the growth of diverse plant life.

Rainforests, such as those found in Dominica and Jamaica, are lush and vibrant, boasting a remarkable diversity of tree species. Towering mahogany, ceiba, and palm trees dominate the canopy, providing shelter for a multitude of animals. Orchids, bromeliads, and ferns adorn the forest floor, creating a captivating tapestry of colors and textures.

Mangrove forests, found in coastal areas throughout the Caribbean, serve as vital nurseries for many marine species. These unique ecosystems feature trees with intricate root systems that extend above the water's surface, creating a complex maze of channels and habitats. Mangroves provide shelter for juvenile fish, crustaceans, and nesting grounds for various bird species.

The Caribbean is home to a remarkable diversity of bird species, with over 560 recorded species inhabiting the region. The vibrant colors and melodious songs of birds such as the Antillean Crested Hummingbird, Jamaican Tody, and Cuban Trogons grace the forests, while graceful herons, egrets, and flamingos can be found in the wetlands and coastal areas.

The Caribbean's waters are teeming with marine life, making it a paradise for snorkelers, divers, and marine enthusiasts. Coral reefs, including the Mesoamerican Barrier Reef in Mexico and the Tobago Cays in the Grenadines, are home to a multitude of fish species. Colorful parrotfish, angelfish, butterflyfish, and damselfish create a vibrant spectacle, while larger species like barracudas and groupers patrol the reefs.

Sea turtles are an iconic part of Caribbean wildlife. Several species, including the green turtle, hawksbill turtle, and leatherback turtle, nest on the region's shores and contribute to the balance of marine ecosystems. These majestic creatures undertake incredible migrations, returning to their birthplaces to lay their eggs, and their presence is a symbol of the Caribbean's commitment to conservation.

The Caribbean is also home to various land-dwelling mammals, although they are less numerous than the region's bird and marine life. Bats, such as the Jamaican fruit bat and the Antillean ghost-faced bat, play an important ecological role as pollinators and seed dispersers. Other notable mammals include the West Indian manatee, which can be spotted in coastal areas, and the Coati, a raccoon-like creature found in some islands.

The islands of the Caribbean are also inhabited by reptiles, including numerous lizard and snake species. The Anolis lizard, known for its ability to change color, is a common sight in gardens and forests. Boa constrictors and non-venomous snakes, such as the Hispaniolan racer, reside in some islands, playing their part in the delicate balance of the ecosystem.

In addition to its diverse fauna, the Caribbean boasts a rich array of plant life. Palm trees, including the iconic coconut palm, dot the landscapes and provide shade on sandy beaches. Tropical fruits such as mangoes, papayas, and bananas thrive in the region's fertile soil, contributing to the vibrant local cuisine. The Caribbean is also known for its medicinal plants and herbs, which have been traditionally used by indigenous peoples for their healing properties. Plants like aloe vera, neem, and moringa are prized for their therapeutic benefits and are still widely utilized today.

Efforts to protect the Caribbean's flora and fauna have gained momentum in recent years, with various conservation initiatives and national parks established throughout the region. These efforts aim to preserve the unique biodiversity of the Caribbean and promote sustainable practices that ensure the long-term survival of its wildlife.

Exploring the wildlife wonders of the Caribbean offers a glimpse into the intricate web of life that thrives in this enchanting region. From the colorful birds that grace the skies to the vibrant marine creatures that inhabit its waters, the Caribbean's flora and fauna captivate the imagination and inspire a sense of wonder and appreciation for the natural world.

Tropical Temptations: Caribbean Cuisine and Drinks

The Caribbean is not only a feast for the eyes with its stunning landscapes and vibrant culture but also a treat for the taste buds with its rich and diverse culinary traditions. This chapter explores the mouthwatering world of Caribbean cuisine and drinks, delving into the unique flavors, ingredients, and cultural influences that have shaped the region's gastronomy.

Caribbean cuisine is a delightful fusion of African, European, Indigenous, and Indian culinary traditions, resulting in a tapestry of flavors that reflects the diverse history and cultural heritage of the islands. Each island boasts its own signature dishes and culinary specialties, making the Caribbean a treasure trove of gastronomic delights.

One of the staples of Caribbean cuisine is seafood. With its vast coastlines and abundant marine resources, the region offers an incredible array of fresh and flavorful seafood options. From succulent lobster and shrimp to delectable fish like snapper and mahi-mahi, seafood dishes are a highlight of Caribbean dining. Grilled, fried, or marinated in zesty citrus flavors, Caribbean seafood showcases the region's coastal bounty.

Rice and beans, known as "rice and peas" in some islands, are a ubiquitous component of Caribbean meals. Prepared with various spices, seasonings, and sometimes coconut milk, this staple dish serves as a delicious accompaniment to many Caribbean meals. It often pairs well with savory meats, such as jerk chicken or pork, adding a comforting and hearty element to the plate.

The Caribbean is renowned for its flavorful and aromatic spice blends, which add depth and complexity to many dishes. Jerk seasoning, a fiery combination of Scotch bonnet peppers, allspice, thyme, and other spices, is a beloved staple. The meat, usually chicken or pork, is marinated in this spicy mixture before being grilled or smoked, resulting in a tantalizing explosion of flavors.

Plantains, a close relative of bananas, play a prominent role in Caribbean cuisine. These starchy fruits are incredibly versatile and can be enjoyed in various forms. Ripe plantains are sweet and are often caramelized or fried to create a delicious side dish or dessert. Green plantains, on the other hand, are used in savory dishes such as tostones (fried plantain slices) or mofongo (mashed plantains with garlic and other seasonings).

In addition to savory dishes, the Caribbean is renowned for its delectable sweets and desserts. One iconic treat is the rum cake, a moist and rich cake infused with Caribbean rum. Coconut is another star ingredient in Caribbean desserts, whether it's in the form of creamy coconut custards, sweet coconut bread, or coconut macaroons.

The Caribbean is also famous for its refreshing and tropical drinks, which provide a delightful respite from the warm climate. Rum, made from sugar cane, is the spirit of choice in the region and forms the base of many beloved Caribbean cocktails. The piña colada, a blend of rum, coconut cream, and pineapple juice, is an iconic Caribbean concoction that transports you to a beachside paradise with a single sip. Other popular Caribbean cocktails include the refreshing Mojito, made with rum, lime, mint, and sugar, and the tangy and fruity Mai Tai, which combines rum, orange liqueur, and tropical juices. Freshly squeezed fruit juices, such as mango, guava, and passionfruit, are also widely enjoyed as non-alcoholic options, offering a burst of natural flavors.

The Caribbean's rich culinary traditions extend to festive occasions and celebrations. Carnival, a vibrant and exuberant festival celebrated throughout the region, showcases the diverse food culture with street food stalls offering a plethora of delicious treats. From savory empanadas and rotis to sweet fritters and coconut candies, Carnival is a feast for all the senses.

The Caribbean's culinary traditions are not limited to its own shores. Caribbean cuisine has influenced global culinary trends, with Caribbean restaurants and flavors gaining recognition worldwide. The fusion of Caribbean and international cuisines has resulted in exciting and innovative dishes that continue to evolve and captivate food enthusiasts around the globe.

Exploring the tropical temptations of Caribbean cuisine and drinks is an invitation to savor the unique flavors, experience the cultural tapestry of the islands, and embark on a culinary journey that celebrates the region's vibrant heritage. Whether enjoying the fiery spices of jerk chicken, sipping on a refreshing rum cocktail, or indulging in a sweet and tropical dessert, Caribbean cuisine offers a sensory adventure that delights and entices.

Caribbean Music and Dance: Soca, Calypso, and Reggaeton

The Caribbean is renowned for its vibrant music and infectious rhythms that have captivated audiences worldwide. This chapter explores the diverse musical genres and dances that have emerged from the Caribbean, including Soca, Calypso, and Reggaeton. These genres represent the unique cultural expressions and rhythmic traditions of the islands, weaving a tapestry of melodies and movements that celebrate the region's rich heritage.

Calypso, originating in Trinidad and Tobago, is a genre deeply rooted in the history and folklore of the Caribbean. It emerged during the colonial era as a means for enslaved Africans to express their emotions, tell stories, and comment on social and political issues. Calypso is characterized by its witty and often humorous lyrics, accompanied by infectious rhythms created by instruments such as steel drums, guitar, and saxophone. Calypso has evolved over the years and continues to be a popular genre, with artists like The Mighty Sparrow and Lord Kitchener gaining international recognition.

Soca, an abbreviation of "soul-calypso," emerged in the 1970s as a fusion of Calypso and various other genres, including funk, soul, and reggae. Soca music is known for its high-energy beats, lively melodies, and joyful lyrics. It is the soundtrack of Caribbean carnivals, igniting the spirit of revelry and celebration. Soca artists like Machel Montano, Destra Garcia, and Bunji Garlin have propelled the genre to global recognition, with their infectious hits and electrifying performances.

Reggaeton, although not originating from the English-speaking Caribbean, has gained significant popularity in the region. It is a genre that originated in Puerto Rico in the late 1990s and is influenced by Jamaican dancehall, hip-hop, and Latin American rhythms. Reggaeton is characterized by its catchy beats, rapid-fire lyrics, and sensual dance moves. Artists like Daddy Yankee, Don Omar, and Bad Bunny have played a significant role in popularizing Reggaeton globally and have brought a distinct Caribbean flavor to the international music scene.

The music of the Caribbean not only reflects the cultural heritage of the region but also serves as a means of storytelling, social commentary, and celebration. It embodies the resilience, creativity, and joy of the Caribbean people, transcending language barriers and connecting people from diverse backgrounds through its infectious rhythms and melodies.

In addition to music, dance plays a vital role in Caribbean culture, serving as a visual expression of the music's energy and passion. Caribbean dance forms are diverse, encompassing traditional folk dances, cultural rituals, and contemporary styles influenced by African, European, and Indigenous traditions.

One iconic Caribbean dance style is the "Limbo," which originated in Trinidad and Tobago. The Limbo involves participants bending backward and gracefully maneuvering under a bar, symbolizing a journey through life's challenges. Other traditional dances include the "Jamaican Quadrille," a lively and colorful folk dance, and the "Merengue," a fast-paced dance originating from the Dominican Republic that embodies the joy and exuberance of the Caribbean spirit.

Caribbean music and dance are not confined to formal performances. They are woven into the fabric of daily life, celebrated at festivals, parties, and social gatherings. The rhythmic beats and infectious melodies inspire spontaneous movement and create a sense of unity and togetherness among participants.

The influence of Caribbean music and dance extends far beyond the islands themselves. Artists from the Caribbean have made significant contributions to global music, influencing genres like reggae, salsa, and hip-hop. The iconic rhythms and dance moves of the Caribbean have become integral parts of popular culture, transcending borders and captivating audiences worldwide.

Exploring the music and dance of the Caribbean is an invitation to experience the vibrant pulse of the islands, to immerse oneself in the lively rhythms and joyful expressions of the region's cultural heritage. From the infectious soca beats that ignite the dance floor to the soulful melodies of Calypso and the fiery energy of Reggaeton, Caribbean music and dance are a celebration of life, a testament to the creativity and spirit of the Caribbean people.

Caribbean Carnival: Festive Celebrations and Masquerades

Caribbean Carnival is a vibrant and exuberant celebration that embodies the spirit and cultural richness of the islands. This chapter explores the history, traditions, and colorful pageantry of Caribbean Carnival, delving into the diverse expressions of this festive event across the region.

Originating from the ancient European tradition of pre-Lenten festivities, Caribbean Carnival has evolved over the centuries, blending with African, Indigenous, and other cultural influences to create a unique and dynamic celebration. It serves as a time of joy, freedom, and creative expression, allowing participants to immerse themselves in a world of music, dance, costumes, and revelry.

The roots of Caribbean Carnival can be traced back to the period of colonialism and slavery. Enslaved Africans used these festivities as an opportunity to momentarily escape the harsh realities of their lives, reclaim their cultural heritage, and express their identities. Through music, dance, and masquerade, they found a space of liberation and resistance, asserting their humanity and cultural pride.

Each Caribbean island has its own distinct Carnival traditions and customs, showcasing the diversity of the region. Trinidad and Tobago's Carnival is renowned as one of the most elaborate and internationally recognized celebrations. It features extravagant costumes, pulsating soca music, and the iconic steelpan, the only acoustic musical instrument invented in the 20th century. The climax of Trinidad and Tobago's Carnival is the two-day street parade known as "The Parade of the Bands," where revelers dance through the streets in a kaleidoscope of colors and sequins.

Other islands such as Barbados, Grenada, Jamaica, and St. Lucia also have their own unique Carnival celebrations, each with its own distinctive character and traditions. In Barbados, the Crop Over festival is a major highlight, culminating in the Grand Kadooment parade, featuring revelers dressed in vibrant costumes, dancing to calypso and soca rhythms. In Grenada, the Spice Mas showcases the island's cultural heritage, with traditional masquerades, energetic soca competitions, and the crowning of a Carnival Queen.

Carnival celebrations typically span several weeks, with various events leading up to the grand finale. Calypso and soca competitions take place, showcasing the lyrical and musical talents of local artists. Participants attend fetes, or lively parties, where they can enjoy live performances, indulge in delicious Caribbean cuisine, and dance the night away.

Masquerade is an integral part of Caribbean Carnival, with participants adorning themselves in vibrant and elaborate costumes, often handmade with meticulous detail. These costumes reflect a range of influences, from historical and mythical characters to contemporary themes and cultural symbols. Feathers, sequins, and vibrant fabrics create a dazzling spectacle as masqueraders parade through the streets, exuding a sense of pride and artistry.

Caribbean Carnival is not only a celebration for locals but also attracts visitors from around the world, drawn by the allure of the festivities. Many Caribbean destinations have embraced Carnival tourism, recognizing the economic and cultural value of this vibrant event. Travelers have the opportunity to immerse themselves in the rhythm and energy of Caribbean Carnival, joining in the revelry, and experiencing the warmth and hospitality of the islands.

Beyond the captivating performances and dazzling costumes, Caribbean Carnival holds deeper cultural significance. It is a space for cultural preservation, where traditions and art forms are passed down from generation to generation. It fosters a sense of community and unity, transcending social barriers and promoting inclusivity and diversity.

The spirit of Caribbean Carnival lives on throughout the year, as communities come together to prepare for the next celebration. Workshops are held to teach the art of costume making, choreography, and music, ensuring the continuity of these vibrant traditions. The legacy of Caribbean Carnival serves as a testament to the resilience, creativity, and cultural pride of the Caribbean people.

Exploring Caribbean Carnival is an invitation to embrace the joy and vibrancy of the islands, to witness the transformative power of celebration and artistic expression. It is an experience that immerses participants in a whirlwind of color, rhythm, and cultural pride, leaving an indelible mark on their hearts and memories. Caribbean Carnival truly embodies the essence of the region, where the past, present, and future converge in a dazzling display of creativity and unity.

Preserving Paradise: Sustainable Tourism in the Caribbean

The Caribbean is renowned for its pristine beaches, crystal-clear waters, and breathtaking natural beauty. As tourism continues to be a major economic driver for the region, there is an increasing focus on sustainable tourism practices that aim to preserve the fragile ecosystems and cultural heritage of the Caribbean. This chapter explores the importance of sustainable tourism in the Caribbean and the various initiatives and strategies implemented to ensure the long-term viability of this paradise.

Sustainable tourism in the Caribbean encompasses a range of practices that prioritize environmental conservation, community engagement, and cultural preservation. It recognizes the interconnectedness of the natural environment, local communities, and the tourism industry, seeking to strike a balance that benefits all stakeholders and protects the region's unique assets.

One of the key aspects of sustainable tourism in the Caribbean is the conservation of the marine and coastal ecosystems. The Caribbean is home to some of the world's most diverse coral reefs, mangrove forests, and seagrass beds, which provide habitat for a vast array of marine life. Efforts are being made to establish marine protected areas, implement responsible diving and snorkeling practices, and reduce pollution and overfishing. These measures aim to ensure the long-term health and resilience of the marine ecosystems that are integral to the Caribbean's allure.

Land-based conservation is also a crucial component of sustainable tourism in the Caribbean. National parks, nature reserves, and botanical gardens have been established to protect the region's unique flora and fauna. Efforts are made to promote responsible hiking, birdwatching, and wildlife viewing, minimizing disturbance to natural habitats and supporting research and conservation initiatives. By preserving the natural landscapes and biodiversity, sustainable tourism aims to provide visitors with authentic and enriching experiences while safeguarding the natural heritage of the Caribbean.

Community engagement and empowerment are fundamental pillars of sustainable tourism in the Caribbean. Local communities are recognized as key stakeholders and are involved in decision-making processes, tourism planning, and the development of tourism-related enterprises. This inclusive approach ensures that the benefits of tourism are shared among the residents, fostering social and economic well-being. Community-based tourism initiatives provide opportunities for visitors to interact with local communities, learn about their traditions and way of life, and contribute to local economies through the purchase of locally made crafts and products.

Cultural preservation is another vital aspect of sustainable tourism in the Caribbean. The region boasts a rich tapestry of cultural traditions, including music, dance, cuisine, and craftsmanship. Efforts are made to promote cultural authenticity and protect traditional knowledge and practices. Cultural heritage sites, museums, and festivals are preserved and showcased to visitors, offering a deeper understanding of the region's history and cultural diversity. By supporting and promoting cultural preservation, sustainable tourism ensures that the Caribbean's cultural heritage remains alive and thriving.

In addition to conservation and community engagement, sustainable tourism in the Caribbean emphasizes responsible resource management and the reduction of the industry's carbon footprint. Eco-friendly practices such as energy and water conservation, waste management, and the use of renewable energy sources are encouraged in hotels, resorts, and other tourism establishments. Efforts are made to minimize the environmental impact of transportation, promote sustainable transportation options, and educate visitors about eco-friendly behaviors during their stay.

Certification programs, such as Green Globe and EarthCheck, play a significant role in promoting and recognizing sustainable tourism practices in the Caribbean. These programs provide guidelines, assessment frameworks, and standards for tourism businesses, ensuring that they meet rigorous sustainability criteria. By achieving certification, businesses demonstrate their commitment to environmental stewardship and social responsibility, instilling confidence in visitors who seek sustainable travel experiences.

The Caribbean's commitment to sustainable tourism is not only driven by environmental and cultural concerns but also by the recognition that sustainable practices are essential for the long-term success and resilience of the tourism industry itself. By preserving the natural beauty and cultural authenticity of the region, the Caribbean ensures that future generations can continue to enjoy its treasures and that tourism remains a sustainable and mutually beneficial endeavor.

In conclusion, sustainable tourism in the Caribbean represents a conscious effort to balance economic development, environmental preservation, and cultural authenticity. By adopting responsible practices, engaging local communities, and promoting conservation, the Caribbean is taking significant strides towards preserving its paradise for generations to come. Sustainable tourism serves as a catalyst for positive change, ensuring that the region's natural wonders and cultural heritage remain intact while providing visitors with meaningful and unforgettable experiences.

Conclusion

The journey through the history, culture, and natural wonders of the Caribbean has been an exploration of a region rich in diversity and captivating stories. From the ancient civilizations that once flourished on these islands to the legacies of colonization and the vibrant expressions of Caribbean identity, each chapter has offered a glimpse into the complexities and beauty of this tropical paradise.

The Caribbean is a tapestry woven with the threads of different cultures, languages, and traditions. It is a place where influences from Africa, Europe, Asia, and the Americas have converged, resulting in a unique blend of music, dance, cuisine, and artistic expressions. The region's history has been shaped by the forces of conquest, slavery, and resistance, leaving indelible marks that continue to shape Caribbean societies today.

The islands of the Caribbean are not only blessed with breathtaking landscapes, but also with an incredible array of flora and fauna. The coral reefs, mangrove forests, and lush rainforests provide habitats for a stunning variety of plant and animal species. It is a haven for birdwatchers, divers, and nature enthusiasts who seek to immerse themselves in the natural wonders of this region.

Tourism has played a significant role in the Caribbean's economic development, offering employment opportunities and driving economic growth. However, the challenges of sustainable tourism loom large, as the delicate balance between preserving the environment, protecting cultural heritage, and meeting the demands of the industry must be carefully managed. The region's commitment to sustainable practices is a testament to its dedication to preserving its natural and cultural treasures for future generations.

As we conclude this journey through the Caribbean, it is important to acknowledge the resilience and strength of the Caribbean people. They have weathered storms, both literal and metaphorical, and have emerged with a vibrant spirit that is evident in their art, music, and everyday life. The stories of the Caribbean are not only tales of struggle and triumph, but also of celebration, creativity, and unity.

The Caribbean is a place that invites exploration, from the idyllic beaches and turquoise waters to the lively streets pulsating with music and dance. It is a destination that captivates the senses and touches the soul. Whether seeking relaxation, adventure, cultural immersion, or simply a moment of respite, the Caribbean offers an abundance of experiences that leave a lasting impression.

As we bid farewell to the Caribbean, let us carry with us the lessons learned, the memories cherished, and the appreciation for the beauty and diversity of this remarkable region. The story of the Caribbean is an ongoing narrative, constantly evolving and shaped by the people who call it home and those who visit its shores. It is a story that will continue to unfold, inviting future generations to discover its wonders and embrace its spirit.

May the spirit of the Caribbean remain alive within us, a reminder of the resilience, creativity, and warmth that define this enchanting corner of the world. Let us continue to celebrate and protect the treasures of the Caribbean, ensuring that its history, culture, and natural wonders endure for generations to come.

Thank you for embarking on this journey through the captivating world of the Caribbean. I hope that the chapters of this book have transported you to sandy beaches, swaying palm trees, and vibrant cultural celebrations.

If you have enjoyed this book and found it informative and engaging, I kindly ask for your support in the form of a positive review. Your review will not only encourage others to explore the wonders of the Caribbean but also help me as a writer to continue sharing captivating stories and insights.

Once again, thank you for joining me on this adventure. Your support and appreciation mean the world to me. May the spirit of the Caribbean stay with you, and may you continue to find inspiration in the wonders of this remarkable region.

Printed in Great Britain
by Amazon